THE 13 MOST IMPORTANT BIBLE LESSONS FOR TEENAGERS

Group

Loveland, Colorado

The 13 Most Important Bible Lessons for Teenagers
Copyright © 1993 Group Publishing, Inc.

Credits
Edited by Michael D. Warden
Designed by Jill Christopher
Cover design by DeWain Stoll
Illustrations by Judy Atwood Bienick

Scripture quotations are from the Holy Bible, New International Version. Copyright © 1973, 1978, 1984 by International Bible Society. Used by permission of Zondervan Publishing House. All rights reserved.

Library of Congress Cataloging-in-Publication Data
The 13 most important Bible lessons for teenagers.
        p.   cm.
     ISBN 1-55945-261-7
     1. Bible—Study and teaching. 2. Christian education of
teenagers.   I. Group Publishing.   II. Title: Thirteen most
important Bible lessons for teenagers.
     BS600.2.A13   1993
     268'.433—dc20   93-13436
                                                                  CIP

13 12 11 10 9 8 7 6   04 03 02 01 00 99 98 97 96

Printed in the United States of America.

Contents

Introduction

"Why did Jesus die on the cross, anyway?" Julia finally voiced the question that raced through most of the other group members' heads. "I mean, why didn't God just wipe out sin and suffering? It doesn't make sense."

Joyce suddenly realized she'd been speaking over kids' heads. She'd been talking about Jesus' final words on the cross, but some of her kids weren't even sure who Jesus is. And they didn't understand a God who'd allow his only son to be brutally killed.

Joyce needed to refocus her meeting—and the next several meetings—to teach kids the basics:

● Who is God?
● Who is Jesus?
● What's a faith commitment?
● What's the church?
● Why do we need a savior?

● ● ●

Kids need a firm faith foundation. They need to know what they believe and why they believe it. Kids who don't know these things are easily swayed by others who challenge their faith or offer them an imitation Christianity.

But many teenagers don't have a strong faith foundation. Even kids who've grown up in the church sometimes can't explain who Jesus is or what it means to be a Christian.

So how do you cover the "basics" of faith with teenagers—and still keep the meetings interesting and fun so kids will really learn?

Use *The 13 Most Important Bible Lessons for Teenagers!* These meetings cover 13 foundational doctrines of Christianity, without boring lectures and endless note-taking. By using active-learning techniques, these fun meetings will hold kids' interest. They'll find it easy to learn

about important Christian doctrines, such as:
- the role of the Holy Spirit in Christians' lives;
- the necessity of prayer;
- the message of Jesus' death and resurrection; and
- the command to tell others about their faith.

The meetings also give a biblical perspective on issues, such as Creation and Jesus' return. And with fast instructions and easy-to-use handouts, you'll be able to help kids learn these vital concepts with ease.

Use these meetings as Sunday school curriculum. Or plan a series of weekly Bible studies that focus on a different topic each week. The meetings work especially well for a confirmation class or a new believers course.

Or you can select certain topics to cover as needs arise in your youth group. For example, in the scene described at the beginning of the Introduction, the youth leader could hold three meetings from the book: "Who Is God?" on page 6, "Who Is Jesus?" on page 21 and "The Family of Faith" on page 60. Each of these meetings gives valuable information about the identity of Christ and his mission here on Earth.

So enjoy *The 13 Most Important Bible Lessons for Teenagers*. And watch your kids' faith blossom as they build a foundation in Christ that'll last forever.

Who Is God?

ay Kesler says many teenagers think getting to heaven is like climbing up through a manhole, with God beating people back through with a baseball bat. The only way people get into heaven is when God turns to look the other way and someone slips by.

Lots of kids have misconceptions about God. Many see him as a severe disciplinarian, only concerned about keeping people in line. Others see him as someone too great and far away to care about "insignificant" humans.

But in the Bible, God has revealed himself to us as a loving and perfect Father. In these times of increasing divorce rates and examples of more and more fathers who hurt their children, kids need a positive model of what a true father is—a father like God. He cares for us better than any earthly father could.

When kids understand God properly as their heavenly father, they can begin to depend on God more and draw closer to him. Use this meeting to help kids develop that understanding.

Objectives

In this meeting kids will:
- care for an egg to help them experience how God cares for us;
- list qualities of the perfect father;
- examine what the Bible says about who God is;
- discuss why they can trust God to care for them; and
- determine areas in which they'll depend on God more.

THE MEETING

1 **Baby Eggbert**—(You'll need an egg and a fine-line marker for each student. If you meet in a room where carpet or something might be damaged by raw eggs, you might want to boil the eggs. However, the activity is more effective with raw ones.)

After all kids enter the meeting room, say: **Today we're going to look at who God really is. But first I'd like each of you to meet someone.**

Give an egg to each teenager and say: **Your egg is going to be your child for this meeting. Carefully draw a face on it, name it and treat it the way a precious child should be treated. You'll want to hold it and keep it warm as much as possible, and obviously you'll want to keep it from getting broken.**

If you're using raw eggs, warn kids of that at this point.

Give kids a few minutes to prepare their eggs, then move on to the next section. At five-minute intervals through the first three sections of the lesson, ask kids how their "children" are doing and remind them of their responsibilities. If an egg gets broken, replace it and debrief the loss of a "child" in activity 4.

2 **World's Greatest Father**—(You'll need a chalkboard and chalk, or newsprint and a marker.)

Say: **Imagine we're a United Nations committee just formed to set up a world's greatest father contest. The first thing we need is a list of qualities a person must have to qualify for the contest. We'll form subcommittees of three to develop that list.**

Form groups of three, and have groups each create a list of at least seven qualities that'd make someone eligible for this contest.

After five minutes, have groups each read their list. Have a volunteer write the qualities on a chalkboard or newsprint as they're read.

From the qualities listed, have kids work together to select the top 10 qualifications from the list. Then ask:

● **Is there any father who fulfills all these qualifications perfectly? Why or why not?** (No, fathers are all human; yes, God does.)

● **How might God be like the perfect father we've described?** (He's wealthy; he's kind; he'd let me have the car every weekend.)

● **How is God unlike the qualities we've listed for the perfect human father?** (He's more powerful; we can't see him.)

Say: **God *is* a lot like the perfect human father. And the father image is one he's chosen to use in describing himself to us. Even though our own earthly fathers aren't perfect, we can learn a lot about God by looking at him as our heavenly father.**

Remember to periodically remind kids about their eggs. Encourage kids to lovingly care for their children.

3 A Proper Introduction—(For each person, you'll need a pencil and a photocopy of the "Introducing . . . God!" handout on page 11.)

Distribute pencils and the "Introducing . . . God!" handouts, and have kids each follow the instructions. If your kids have extremely limited biblical knowledge, have them work in groups of three to complete the handout. Otherwise, have kids work alone.

When kids have finished their handouts, have several volunteers read what they came up with. There are many good possibilities, but here's what someone might write:

Hi, I'm <u>Paul</u>, and I'm here to introduce you to my father. He's <u>generous</u> and <u>giving</u>, and he really likes to <u>give me good things</u>. He likes it when I <u>obey him</u>, and I enjoy being <u>his child</u>. I especially like him because he <u>made</u> me and <u>takes care of</u> me. I know he'll never <u>treat me bad</u>, and I know I can always count on him because he <u>loves me</u>. His love for me is <u>going to last forever</u>! I now present to you . . . God!

Once God has had this proper introduction to your group, ask:

● **Why can we be sure God wants good things for us?** (He's the best father we could possibly have; he wants us to be happy.)

● **How might God feel when we make choices that aren't the best for us?** (Rejected; sad; hurt.)

● **How does God feel when we respond to him in love by obeying him?** (Glad; relieved; excited.)

Say: **As our perfect heavenly father, God wants what's best for us. He made us and he wants to take care of us. And he wants us to show how much we love him by following what he tells us in the Bible.**

Baby Eggbert Revisited—(No materials needed.)

Say: **You've been caring for your child now for quite a while. How's everyone doing?**

After kids respond, ask:

● **Suppose your child did something you didn't like—like rolling across the table away from you. Would you grab your child and crush it in your hand? Why or why not?**

● **What *would* you do instead?** (Gently pick it up; roll it back where it belonged.)

● **Some people think God is waiting to crush us when we do wrong. Do you think God, as our heavenly father, would delight in crushing us like eggs? Explain.** (No, he cares about us; no, but he may punish us.)

● **What do you think he'd do if we did something wrong?** (Gently bring us back where we need to be; help us see how we need him.)

Eggbert and Me—(You'll need a Bible. For each person, you'll need a 2×4-inch slip of paper and a pencil.)

Have someone read aloud 1 Peter 5:6-7. Say: **If God is the all-powerful creator and he loves us and cares about us so much, we certainly can trust him to help us. Choose an area in your life where you need to depend on his help more. It might be your future, school problems, relationships—or something else. Then think about what you'll do to begin depending on him more in that area.**

Give kids each a slip of paper and a pencil, and have them each write the area they've chosen and how they'll depend on God more.

When kids each have written something on their paper, form pairs. Have partners each tell what they've written and how they plan to start trusting God more in that area. Have partners each respond by encouraging their partner with words such as, "I appreciate your love for God, and I know he'll help you when you depend on him."

All the King's Children—(For each person, you'll need a plastic egg and a fine-line marker.)

Gather all the egg "children," and pass out plastic eggs to everyone. Have kids each write their name on their plastic egg. Have kids each fold their slip of paper from activity 5 and put it inside their plastic egg. Then have kids each stand in a circle and hold their plastic egg.

Say: **When we have faith in Christ, we're all God's children—as your eggs were your children through this session. And God will take care of us even more carefully than you cared for your eggs.**

Close with prayer. Thank God for loving us, and ask him to help your kids follow through on trusting him more.

Encourage kids each to keep their plastic egg in a prominent place at home to remind them of God's love and care for them.

by Paul Woods

Introducing ...God!

Read each of the Bible passages to the right. Then fill in the missing words or phrases in the introduction. There are no right answers. Fill in anything you think fits based on the passages you've read.

Jeremiah 31:3

Matthew 7:9-11

Acts 17:24-29

Ephesians 1:3-5

HI! I'm _____ and I am here to introduce you to my heavenly father. He's _____ and _____, and he really _____.

likes to _____ He likes it when I _____, and I enjoy being _____. I especially like him because he _____ me and me.

I know he'll never _____ and I know I can always count on him because he _____. His love for me is _____!

I now present to you ...GOD!

What is the Bible?

t's too hard to read."

"It's too much information to sift through."

"It doesn't apply to my life."

Kids can find lots of reasons not to read the Bible. But underneath most of their excuses lies one consistent theme: "The Bible intimidates me."

God never intended for the Bible to be intimidating. It's the most important way God reveals himself to those who've made a faith commitment to Jesus Christ. Young people, especially, need the guidance the Bible can give them—guidance for relationships, purpose in life, and love. But they'll never get that guidance if they never open the book.

God wants to relate to young people through his Word and show them how they can relate to God. Use this meeting to relieve kids' apprehension about the Bible and help them see how God reveals himself through his Word.

Objectives

In this meeting kids will:

- explore what the Bible says about itself;
- learn the story of the Bible;
- discover the importance of scripture reading; and
- create a plan for daily Bible reading.

THE MEETING

1 **Book Mixer**—(For each person, you'll need a piece of tape and a 3×5 card with a famous book title written on it. Some examples are *War and Peace*, *Huckleberry Finn*, *The Grapes of Wrath*, *Animal Farm*, *Moby Dick* and *A Tale of Two Cities*. It's okay to use a title more than once, but use as many different titles as possible.)

On each young person's back, tape one 3×5 card with a famous book title written on it. Instruct kids each to mill around the room asking yes-or-no questions about the identity of their book. Kids can answer only with "yes" and "no." Tell kids they can ask no more than two questions of any one person.

After kids discover the identity of their books, have them each put their card on the front of their shirt. Ask:

● **Why are these books so famous?** (Because they're written by famous people; because they're good books.)

● **What qualities have helped these books endure over the years?** (They tell neat stories; they're well-written.)

Say: **Today we'll look at the best-selling book of all time— the Bible. We'll see why it's so well-known and why it has endured through the years.**

2 **Station Revelation**—(Set up five stations around the room, each supplied with a Bible open to one of these scriptures: Station #1—2 Timothy 3:16-17; Station #2—Hebrews 4:12; Station #3—Psalm 119:105; Station #4—James 1:22-24; and Station #5—John 1:1-2, 14. For each person, you'll need a pencil and a photocopy of the "Station Revelations" handout on page 17.)

Form five groups. A group can be one person. Number groups 1 through 5. Give kids each a pencil and a "Station Revelations" handout.

Say: **Complete your handout by going to each of the five stations and reading the assigned scriptures. The Bibles are already open to the passages you need to read. Here's how you use the Bible references listed on your handout to find the verses in the Bible:**

Look at the reference. The first word you'll see is the

book title, such as "Psalm" or "John." Following the title you'll see a number with a colon after it. That number indicates the chapter of the book you want. Look in your open Bible and locate where that chapter begins.

After the colon you'll see another number or series of numbers. These indicate specific verses within the chapter. Verses in the Bible are numbered in order. Locate the verses within the chapter that you're to read.

Have kids start at the station that corresponds to the number of their group. Then have kids go to the other stations until their handout is complete.

When everyone has been to all the stations, go over the handouts in the large group. Have volunteers share what they discovered about the Bible. Then ask:

● **How is going from station to station like learning from the Bible in real life?** (Just as we went from one station to the next, so the Bible guides us from one step in life to the next; each time we study the Bible, we discover something new that gives us a new direction to go in life.)

● **What's one way you can start learning more about God and life from the Bible?** (I can start reading it regularly; I can memorize verses that help me.)

Bible Acts—(You'll need the "Bible Story" on pages 18 and 19.)

Say: **The Bible is actually a collection of many different books. For example, the Table of Contents identifies two testaments or "binding agreements between God and his people"—old and new. Also, there are 39 books listed in the Old Testament and 27 books listed in the New Testament for a total of 66. But even though there are so many books, they all work together to tell one story—the story of God revealing himself to people. Let's act out major stories from the Bible to get a better idea of how God reveals himself through his Word.**

Using the "Bible Story," assign all the parts listed in the instructions. Tell kids each to act out their part in the story as you read the story aloud. For example, when you read "God created Adam and Eve," have "God" pretend to create "Adam" and "Eve."

After reading the story, ask:

● **What surprised you about this story?** (That it all flowed together so well; that it's so easy to understand.)

● **What's important about this story?** (It tells how God revealed himself to us; it tells about Jesus.)

● **Why should we learn the stories in the Bible?** (Because they teach us lessons about how to live; because they tell us about God.)

 Eye-Catching Scriptures—(You'll need a sheet of paper. For each person, you'll need a pencil and a photocopy of the "Scripture-Reading Covenant" on page 20.) Ask:

● **What Bible stories would you like to hear again or learn more about?**

● **What's one question you have about the Bible?**

Share with your young people your own values about reading the Bible. Answer these questions to help get you started:

● When did the Bible become important to you?

● What value do you place on daily scripture reading?

● In what ways do you struggle with reading the Bible?

● When do you read?

● What version do you read?

● How does the Bible guide you through problems and tough decisions?

● How do you apply what you read to your life?

Give kids each a pencil and a "Scripture-Reading Covenant."

Say: **A covenant is like a contract. It can be an agreement between two people or between God and a person or group. In the Bible, it was considered a serious binding agreement—broken only by the death of one of the parties.**

Give kids each time to read through their covenant and make a plan for their own reading. You may want to supplement this covenant with reading plans that assign certain books or chapters to each day or week of the year so kids can go through the entire Bible within a year or two. Ask your local Christian bookseller for samples.

Have kids form pairs and pray with their partners for God's grace to help them keep their new covenant. Encourage kids each to keep their covenant in the front of their Bible.

On a sheet of paper, have kids each write their name and phone number. Tell kids that in a month, you'll be calling them to see how their Bible reading is going and remind them of their covenant. File the sheet where you'll remember to call the kids in a month.

5 Undercover Affirmations—(No supplies needed.)
Have kids form a circle. Say: **We all know the adage, "You can't tell a book by its cover." That's true of the Bible and people. Share something positive about the person on your right that people might not see unless they looked beyond his or her "cover."**

Go around the circle, and have kids each share about the person on their right.

6 Thankful Closings—(No supplies needed.)
Have kids stay in the circle. Instruct kids each to think of a sentence that expresses thanks to God for something they've learned about the Bible. For example, kids might say, "Thanks for letting me see your love through the Bible" or "Thanks for giving me direction in life through your Word."

After everyone has spoken, close with a brief prayer thanking God for the Bible and all it offers us.

by Scott C. Noon

STATION *Revelations*

During the next few minutes, you'll have the chance to wander through five stations, each displaying one of the scriptures listed below. Each scripture has something to say about the Bible and what it means to us as Christians. As you stop at each station, think of what the scripture says about the Bible. Then follow the instructions below. After you've been to all five stations, return to your seat.

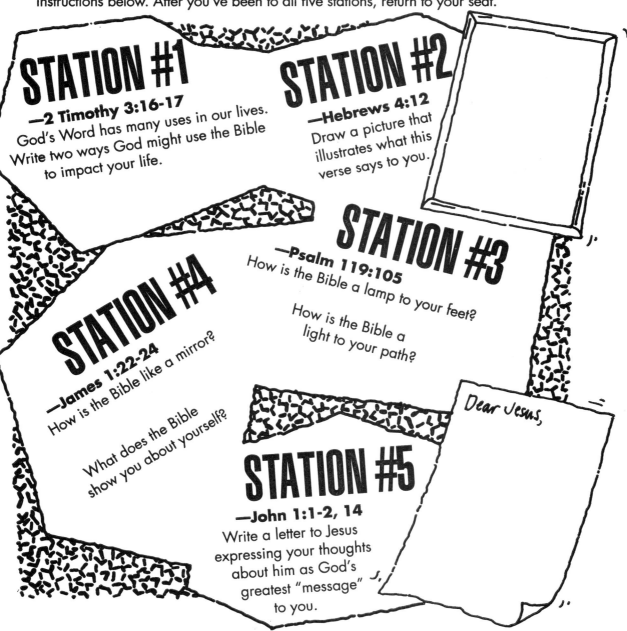

STATION #1

—2 Timothy 3:16-17

God's Word has many uses in our lives. Write two ways God might use the Bible to impact your life.

STATION #2

—Hebrews 4:12

Draw a picture that illustrates what this verse says to you.

STATION #3

—Psalm 119:105

How is the Bible a lamp to your feet?

How is the Bible a light to your path?

STATION #4

—James 1:22-24

How is the Bible like a mirror?

What does the Bible show you about yourself?

STATION #5

—John 1:1-2, 14

Write a letter to Jesus expressing your thoughts about him as God's greatest "message" to you.

Dear Jesus,

BIBLE STORY

Before you read this story aloud, assign each of the following parts to kids. It's okay if one person has more than one part. But if you do ask someone to do two characters, assign parts that don't interact, such as Adam and Jesus, or Noah and Christians.

Characters: God, Adam, Eve, Noah, Abraham, Israel, the Promised Land, Jesus, apostles and Christians.

Long ago, God created the world (pause to let God create the world). **Then he created Adam and Eve** (pause to let God create Adam and Eve), **but they rebelled against him** (pause to let Adam and Eve rebel against God) **and were banished from God's presence** (pause to let Adam and Eve hide from God).

As more and more people were born into the world, the world became more and more wicked. Finally, God decided to flood the Earth and start over (pause to let God flood the Earth). **But God saved one man—Noah—because he alone believed in God. Noah built an ark to carry him and his family through the storm** (pause to let Noah sail through the storm).

One of Noah's descendants—Abraham—became the father of a great nation, Israel (pause to let Abraham act like a father to Israel). **Eventually, God led Israel to a beautiful Promised Land, and it became Israel's home** (pause to let God lead Israel to the Promised Land).

Israel went through many struggles and victories in the centuries that followed (pause to let Israel act this out). **But even through its**

(continued on next page)

struggles, Israel hoped that one day God would send a savior who'd bring peace forever (pause to let Israel hope in God).

When the time was right, God did send a savior—his son Jesus (pause to let God send Jesus to Israel). **Jesus was God in human form. He told people about God's love and peace** (pause to let Jesus tell about God's love and peace). **He also told people about their sin and their need for repentance** (pause to let Jesus tell about people's sin and their need for repentance).

Although many people believed Jesus, most rejected him. They sentenced Jesus to die on a cross (pause to let Jesus die on a cross). **Three days after his death, Jesus rose from the dead** (pause to let Jesus rise from the dead). **By doing this, Jesus broke down the wall between God and his people because of Adam's and Eve's sin** (pause to let Jesus break down a wall). **Then Jesus sent the apostles into all the world to share the message of Jesus' life and purpose with others** (pause to let the apostles go into all the world). **Jesus returned to heaven to be with God** (pause to let Jesus return to God).

Jesus will return again to take all Christians with him to heaven (pause to let Jesus return to gather Christians to heaven). **And all people who believe in Jesus as their Lord and Savior will be with God forever** (pause to let everyone huddle around God).

The End

Scripture-Reading Covenant

This covenant is between God and

_____

Because my relationship with God is important to me and because God desires to continue to teach and inspire me, I commit myself to the following plan for scripture reading:

Goals I want to reach:

Example: I'll read the Bible for 20 minutes each day.
I'll read the entire Bible over the next year.

I'll . . .

My plan for reaching these goals:

Example: I'll set aside 20 minutes each day after school for
reading the Bible.
I'll finish the Old Testament by September and read
the New Testament in the fall.

I'll . . .

Signed: _____

Date: _____

Who Is Jesus?

ho is Jesus, anyway? How do you define him for teenagers who have little knowledge of the Bible or no
experience in the Christian faith? How about . . .
● Jesus is God's son.

● Jesus was more than a prophet.

● Jesus was a good man who helped a lot of people. We should
model our lives after him.

● Jesus was an amazing guy who lived a long time ago. And people
still talk about him today.

No matter how you describe Jesus, kids need to understand the
God-man our Christian faith is based on. Jesus is what Christianity is
all about.

Use this meeting to teach kids about who Jesus is, what he did and
why he's so important in our lives today.

Objectives

In this meeting kids will:

● list what they already know about Jesus;
● search the Bible for descriptions and facts about Jesus;
● use "If . . . then" statements to apply their knowledge to their
  lives today;
● design wanted posters of themselves; and
● receive a reminder of Jesus' love for them.

THE MEETING

1 **Wanted—a Definition of Jesus**—(You'll need a photocopy of the "Wanted" poster on page 27, enlarged to 11×17 inches if possible. Tape the poster to a wall. For each person, you'll need a pencil and two large sticky labels.)

As kids enter the meeting room, give them each a pencil and two large sticky labels. Show the "Wanted" poster, and have kids each write on their labels what they already know about Jesus. It can be as simple as "He was a man" or "He lived a long time ago."

After kids have written their answers and stuck them to the poster, read aloud kids' statements. Then say: **We're going to add to what we already know about Jesus and apply it to our lives today. We're all "private eyes" in search of a most-wanted man: Jesus.**

2 **Mystery Theater**—(You'll need a manger. If you don't have a manger, use a box filled with hay or straw and label it "Manger." You'll also need as many of the following "Sherlock Holmes" props as you can get: a hat, a trench coat, a pipe and a magnifying glass.)

Put on the Sherlock Holmes outfit, and walk over to the manger. Say in your best British accent: **Welcome to Mystery Theater. We are in search of a most-wanted man: a man named Jesus. But what do we know about this person? How do we solve the case of his identity? Let's look at facts we already know about his birth and early years.**

Fact #1—His mother was the Virgin Mary, his earthly father was Joseph. He's God's son. Most amazing facts, and you can read about them in Luke 1:26-35.

Fact #2—Jesus was born in a small town called Bethlehem. He was born in a manger like this, because there wasn't room for his parents to stay in any of the town's inns (Luke 2:1-7).

Fact #3—Angels and a star led shepherds and wise men to see the baby Jesus. They'd been waiting for this amazing moment. Prophets from ages before had predicted Jesus' birth (Matthew 2:1-12 and Luke 2:8-20).

Fact #4—Twelve-year-old Jesus astonished religious teachers in the temple with his knowledge about God (Luke 2:41-52).

Fact #5—Jesus began his ministry when he was about 30 years old (Luke 3:23).

Say: **And here ends our Mystery Theater. Let's continue our search for other clues to this man's identity.**

3 **Jesus Clues**—(For every two people, you'll need a Bible, a marker and a photocopy of the "Clue Search" handout on page 28.)

Form pairs by having kids, one at a time, either say "Sherlock" or "Watson." Have the "Sherlocks" each find a "Watson" for a partner.

Give each mystery-solving duo a Bible, a marker and a "Clue Search" handout. Tell the pairs the clues they'll analyze are found in the Bible. Kids may be unfamiliar with the Bible. If so, have everyone use the same Bible translation and give kids the page numbers where their verses are found.

Have pairs each look up one or more of the following passages and write one fact about Jesus on their handout. Depending on the number of kids you have, you may need to give more than one passage to each pair so all the passages are covered. Here are the passages and clues:

● Matthew 2:4-6 (Prophets predicted God would send a savior. Jesus fulfills that prediction or prophecy.)

● Matthew 3:17 (Jesus is God's son.)

● Matthew 6:8-15 (Jesus teaches us how to pray to God.)

● Matthew 8:26-27 (Jesus did many miracles and amazed many people.)

● Matthew 28:20b (Jesus promises to be with us forever.)

● John 3:16-17 (God loves us so much he sent Jesus to live and die for us. If we believe in him, we'll live forever.)

● John 14:6 (Jesus is the only way to be with God. Jesus is truth. Jesus is life.)

● 1 John 3:16 (Because of Jesus' example, we know how to love each other.)

When pairs are finished, have them each tell what they wrote on their handout. Congratulate the pairs on their investigative prowess.

4 **Brilliant Deductions, Watsons**—(You'll need a marker and a sheet of newsprint taped to the wall. At the top of the newsprint write, "If we know ..." In the middle of the newsprint write, "Then we know ..." You'll also need tape.)

Have kids stay with their partners. Say: **Now that you've searched for clues, we're going to test your "private eye-Qs." For all the facts we learned, we'll come up with ideas of what they mean for us today.**

Call kids' attention to the newsprint on the wall.

Have pairs each come to the front of the room one at a time and read the fact about Jesus they wrote on their "Clue Search" handout. Have pairs each tape their handout to the newsprint under "If we know ..."

Then, as a large group, complete and write an example of "Then we know ..." For example,

If we know ...
Jesus died for our sins because he loves us.
Then we know ...
We're important to him.

Write kids' responses under "Then we know."

Continue until all the handouts are taped to the newsprint and you've written an example of what each fact means. Then ask:

● **How is our private-eye search like our search to find meaning in life?** (We use facts to draw conclusions about how we should live; we base what we do on what we know.)

● **How would the conclusions we've drawn here affect the way you live if you lived by them all the time?** (I wouldn't worry about anything; I'd love people a lot more.)

● **What's one conclusion that especially affects you? Explain.**

● **How will that conclusion change the way you live?**

5 **You're Wanted**—(You'll need an instant-print camera and film. For each person, you'll need construction paper, a marker and tape. If you don't have an instant-print camera, have kids draw pictures of each other on white paper.)

Say: **As you've deducted from your private-eye search, Jesus loves each of you, and he wants to be the center of your lives. Jesus wants you.**

Take an instant-print picture of each person. Give kids each their picture and a marker. Have them each tape their picture to the center of a sheet of construction paper. At the top, have kids each write, "Wanted." At the bottom, have kids each write, "Jesus wants (young person's name) because he loves (him or her) very much." Have kids each tape their picture around the "Wanted" poster of Jesus.

6 Case Closed—(You'll need a marker. Photocopy and cut apart enough of the "Cross Patterns" on page 29 so each person has one. Gather five different-size sacks, and put the crosses in the smallest sack. Number the sacks from largest to smallest, and on each sack write one of Jesus' affirmations from below. Place the sacks inside each other, starting with the smallest and ending with the largest—so everything ends up in the largest sack.)

Write these affirmations from Jesus on the sacks:

● **Bag #1**—"Indeed, the very hairs of your head are all numbered. Don't be afraid; you are worth more than many sparrows" (Luke 12:7).

● **Bag #2**—"Do not be afraid, little flock, for your Father has been pleased to give you the kingdom" (Luke 12:32).

● **Bag #3**—"I give them eternal life, and they shall never perish; no one can snatch them out of my hand" (John 10:28).

● **Bag #4**—"Peace I leave with you; my peace I give you. I do not give to you as the world gives. Do not let your hearts be troubled and do not be afraid" (John 14:27).

● **Bag #5**—"You did not choose me, but I chose you and appointed you to go and bear fruit—fruit that will last. Then the Father will give you whatever you ask in my name" (John 15:16).

Form a circle, and show kids the large sack (with the other sacks inside it). Pass around the sack while having kids sing, "Jesus loves me, this I know." When the song phrase ends, have the person holding the sack read aloud the affirmation on the sack. Then remove the outer sack and continue passing while kids say the words again. Continue until all five affirmations are read. Have the person who opens the smallest sack present a cross to each person.

Encourage kids each to keep their cross on their bathroom mirror or in their school locker as a daily reminder of Jesus' love.

Encourage kids to learn more about Jesus' life, death and Resurrection by reading the Gospels: Matthew, Mark, Luke and John.

7 **Celebrating a Solved Case**—(You'll need refreshments.)

Celebrate the private eyes' excellent work by serving goodies such as:
- detective doughnuts,
- case-closed Kool-Aid, and
- brilliant-deduction bubble gum.

by Cindy Hansen

WANTED:

The identity of this man.

Those who help identify him will receive a
—REWARD—

CLUE SEARCH

Write your clue to Jesus' identity in the magnifying glass.

Cross Patterns

Photocopy and cut apart these crosses.

Who Is the Holy Spirit?

To kids, the Holy Spirit can seem like Casper the friendly ghost—something teenagers can't see but like having around. Putting the Holy Spirit into words is difficult, but watching what the Spirit does can make him evident.

Rather than a vaporlike ghostly thing, the Holy Spirit is God. The Holy Spirit knows the mind of God and communicates God to our minds, hearts and actions (John 16:13-15).

The Holy Spirit has many functions: fruit-producer, counselor, comforter and convictor (John 14:15-17; John 16:7-11; and Galatians 5:22-23). The Holy Spirit is the Christian's on-site, personal guide to fulfilled living. The Holy Spirit doesn't always insulate us from illness, tragedy or pain, but always comforts and empowers Christians during those times.

Teenagers need power to handle tough situations and to make good happen. Use this meeting to help your group recognize the superiority of the Holy Spirit's power and to teach them how the Holy Spirit fits into their lives.

Objectives
In this meeting kids will:
- identify the Holy Spirit as a part of the Trinity;
- pinpoint several of the Holy Spirit's functions;
- recognize that the Holy Spirit is for all Christians;
- play a game to remember the fruit of the Spirit; and
- discuss how the Holy Spirit's power is superior to any other.

THE MEETING

1 **Divine Trinity—**(You'll need an ice cube, a glass of water and a steaming cup of recently boiled water.)
   Display an ice cube, a glass of water and a steaming cup of recently boiled water. Ask:
● **Which is God most like? Explain.** (Ice, because he's solid; water, because he refreshes people.)
● **What do ice, water and steam have in common?** (They're all made of water; they all have the same chemical formula.)
● **How are they different?** (They look totally different from each other; they all exist at different temperatures.)
   Say: **God is like this in a way. He functions in three ways—Father, Son (Jesus) and the Holy Spirit. These three aspects of God together are called the Trinity.**
   Ask:
● **How does the word "Trinity" help you understand God?** (The word reminds me there are three elements; it gives me a unified picture of God.)

2 **What Does the Holy Spirit Do?—**(You'll need a photocopy of the "God Acts" handout on page 35, cut apart and placed inside a lunch-size paper sack. You'll also need music and something to play it on.)
   Form a circle. Show the sack of "God Acts," and say: **This bag contains descriptions of God's actions. We'll play a game to determine which person of the Trinity does what. Remember that some actions are shared by the whole Trinity.**
   Play music, and have kids pass the sack around the circle without looking inside. Stop the music at random intervals. Each time you stop the music, have the person holding the bag draw out one action and read it aloud. Then brainstorm as a group which person of the Trinity does that action.
   Point out that distinguishing between functions isn't always smooth because the three are really one. Say: **Although many functions are shared by the Trinity, a few are done specifically by the Holy Spirit. Let's discover what those functions are.**

Use these answers to "God Acts" and supporting scripture references to help kids discover the best choice:

1. All (Genesis 1:1-2, 26)
2. Jesus (John 1:14)
3. Holy Spirit (John 14:26)
4. All (Psalm 90:2)
5. Holy Spirit (John 16:8-10)
6. Holy Spirit (John 16:8-9)
7. Holy Spirit (John 14:16)
8. Holy Spirit (John 16:13-15)
9. Jesus (Romans 5:6-8)
10. Father, Jesus (1 John 1:9)
11. Father (Matthew 24:36; Hebrews 4:13)

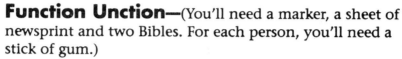 **Function Unction**—(You'll need a marker, a sheet of newsprint and two Bibles. For each person, you'll need a stick of gum.)

Write the following description on a sheet of newsprint. The Holy Spirit:

● lives within Christians to guide them;
● convicts Christians when they do wrong;
● guides Christians to do right;
● comforts Christians; and
● helps Christians understand God.

Don't let kids see the newsprint yet. Form two teams, and give them each a Bible. Have teams each read aloud John 14:16-17 and John 16:5-15. Have teams race to discover from the passages each function you listed on the hidden newsprint. Have the teams yell "Function!" each time they find what they think is one of the functions you listed. Continue until kids guess all the functions you listed.

When groups are finished, have everyone look at the newsprint to check answers, and give kids each a stick of gum for their efforts.

How Do You Know the Holy Spirit Is There?—(For every four people, you'll need a set of "Fruit Slap Cards" on pages 36 and 37, and a Bible.)

Read aloud Ephesians 1:13-14. Say: **Although the Holy Spirit is at work in people's lives from the beginning, the Holy Spirit comes to live *within* Christians the moment they each become a Christian, and the Holy Spirit stays there to guide, comfort, counsel and convict.**

Ask:

● **How do you know an apple tree from a pear tree?** (By

the way it looks; by the fruit it produces.)

● **How do you know a good friend from a bad friend?** (By how he or she treats you; by the company he or she keeps.)

● **How do you tell whether people have the Holy Spirit living within?** (By the way they live; they believe in God.)

Say: **Learning about the Holy Spirit is similar to learning about trees and friends. The Holy Spirit produces fruit in a Christian's life just as trees are known by their fruit or friends by their actions.**

To help kids learn different aspects of the Holy Spirit's fruit, have them play Fruit Slap.

Form groups of four or fewer. Have groups each sit in a circle. Give groups each a shuffled deck of "Fruit Slap Cards" and a Bible. Have groups each open their Bible to Galatians 5:22-23 and place the deck face down in the middle of the circle.

Have group members each take turns turning over the top card in the deck. Instruct kids that if the card reveals a fruit of the Spirit, they each must try to slap their hand on the card before anyone else. The first person to slap the card keeps it. Kids who each slap a card that isn't a fruit of the spirit must place one of their fruit cards back into the deck. If those kids don't have any fruit cards yet, have them each place the first card they win back in the deck.

After the game, have kids each choose one fruit of the Spirit from Galatians 5:22-23 and tell how it would help other people see God in them. Ask:

● **If a Christian doesn't show these fruits, is the Holy Spirit present in his or her life? Why or why not?** (Maybe, but that Christian is hiding him; no, the Holy Spirit stays with all Christians.)

Say: **The Holy Spirit lives in every Christian, but not all Christians let the Holy Spirit work. Christians choose daily whether to let the Holy Spirit produce fruit.**

5 How Does the Holy Spirit's Power Work?—

(For each person, you'll need several pipe cleaners.)

Give kids each several pipe cleaners, and have them each create a sculpture that represents power.

When everyone is finished, have kids each explain their sculpture. Ask kids how each sculpture is or isn't like the Holy Spirit's power. Some possible answers might be:

● The Holy Spirit's power is like a world leader's power, because he can control many people; it's not like a world leader's power, because the Holy Spirit doesn't force himself on people.

● The Holy Spirit's power is like lightning because people can't control where and when it will come.

● The Holy Spirit's power is like electricity because it energizes people to love others and obey God—something they can't do effectively on their own.

Say: **The Holy Spirit has power greater than any other power, power that can solve any problem or enhance any joy.**

Ask:

● **How is the Holy Spirit's power greater than military force?** (It could wipe out any military force in a second; it operates on love rather than fear.)

● **How is the Holy Spirit's power greater than money?** (Money can't bring happiness, but the Holy Spirit can; money just surrounds you with neat things, but the Holy Spirit fills you on the inside.)

● **How is the Holy Spirit's power greater than a political office?** (Politicians make mistakes, but the Holy Spirit doesn't; the Holy Spirit can change people's hearts, but politicians can just pass laws to control people's actions.)

● **How does the Holy Spirit use his power to guide you?** (He talks to you in your spirit; he affects circumstances to make your path clear.)

6 **Power Provision—**(For each person, you'll need a Bible.)

Say: **The Holy Spirit's power is great, but it's available to everyone who truly wants it. The way to tap into the Holy Spirit's power is to become a Christian. Once you make a faith commitment to Christ, God comes to live within you in the person of the Holy Spirit.**

Ask:

● **What are the benefits of becoming a Christian?** (You gain the ability to do what's right; you experience God's love and power through the Holy Spirit.)

● **What are the benefits of having the Holy Spirit guide your life?** (You don't have to go through bad times alone; you have direction in life.)

Say: **You'll experience God's power as you let the Holy**

Spirit teach you about God and produce fruit such as love, joy, peace, patience and faithfulness.

Have kids each read Galatians 5:22-23. Form a circle and say: **As a closing, say one fruit of the Spirit you see in the person on your right and how you see that fruit demonstrated. For example, "I see the fruit of peace in Mark's life because nothing really seems to upset him."**

After everyone has spoken, close with prayer by thanking God for sending the Holy Spirit to live in us.

by Karen Dockrey

God Acts

Photocopy and cut apart these strips, then fold and place each in a lunch-size sack.

1. Created the Earth

2. Came to live on Earth as a human

3. Lives with Christians to guide them

4. Always was and always will be

5. Convicts Christians to do right

6. Convicts people of sin

7. Comforts Christians

8. Helps Christians know God

9. Died for our sins

10. Forgives Christians when they turn from their sin and ask forgiveness

11. All-knowing, all-present

FRUIT SLAP CARDS

Photocopy and cut apart a set of these cards for every four people. The words on the cards are taken from Galatians 5:19-23 (NIV).

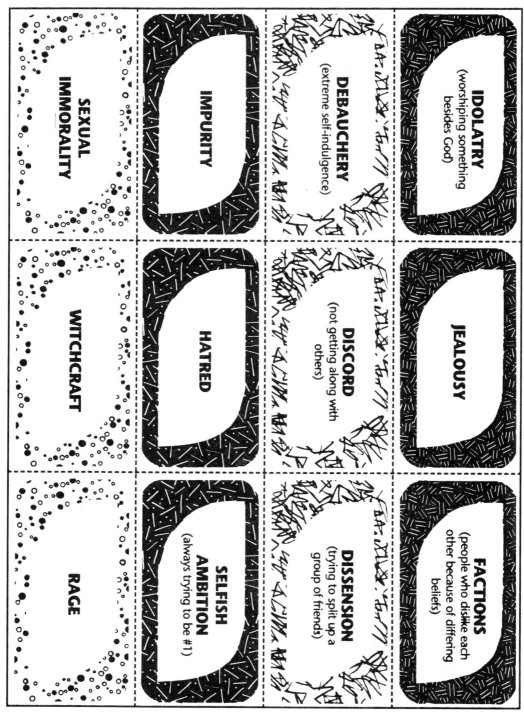

SEXUAL IMMORALITY

IMPURITY

DEBAUCHERY
(extreme self-indulgence)

IDOLATRY
(worshiping something besides God)

WITCHCRAFT

HATRED

DISCORD
(not getting along with others)

JEALOUSY

RAGE

SELFISH AMBITION
(always trying to be #1)

DISSENSION
(trying to split up a group of friends)

FACTIONS
(people who dislike each other because of differing beliefs)

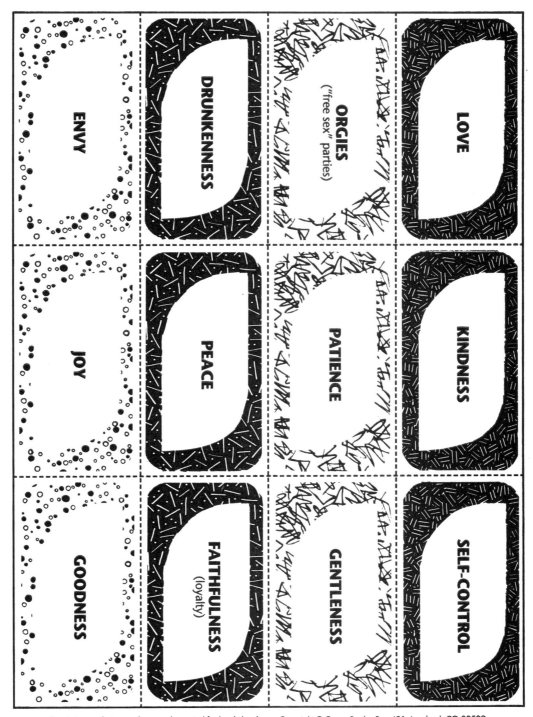

ENVY

DRUNKENNESS

ORGIES
("free sex" parties)

LOVE

JOY

PEACE

PATIENCE

KINDNESS

GOODNESS

FAITHFULNESS
(loyalty)

GENTLENESS

SELF-CONTROL

In the Beginning

Teenagers wonder about creation. They wonder how our planet, the stars and humanity fit together. They wonder if their lives have significance.

God created our world. God created us and breathed life into our lungs. We were made caretakers of creation. We were fashioned to live in harmony with God, self, others and nature. Use this meeting to help kids see their place in creation and their role on the Earth.

Objectives

In this meeting kids will:
- act out the creation story;
- compare the creation stories;
- identify important themes in Genesis 1—2;
- experience being tied to creation; and
- celebrate God's gift of creation.

THE MEETING

1 Clay Creations—(For each person, you'll need Play-Doh or modeling clay.)

Hand each person Play-Doh or modeling clay. Say: **Imagine God has just handed you this glob of formless material. Shape something from nature that you particularly like.**

For example, you might shape a flower, tree, bird or animal.

After everyone is finished, have kids each explain their creation and tell why they chose it. Ask:

● **What was difficult about beginning with a formless mass?** (I didn't know what to make; it was hard to create anything without a model.)

● **How'd you decide what to create?** (I thought of something I liked; I thought of something simple.)

● **What's special about your object?** (I made it; it represents a part of my personality.)

● **How is your creating something out of clay like God creating the world?** (Creation is an expression of God's personality; God's creation is important to him.)

Say: **Sometimes we wonder how our world and all its beauty got here. Let's look in Genesis 1—2 for some clues.**

2 Start From the Beginning—(For each person, you'll need a Bible.)

Form six groups. A group can be one person. If you have fewer than six kids, give more than one scripture passage to some kids. Give kids each a Bible, and assign them each one (or more) of these scriptures: Genesis 1:3-5; Genesis 1:6-8; Genesis 1:9-13; Genesis 1:14-19; Genesis 1:20-23; and Genesis 1:24-31.

Say: **Each group has one day in God's creative process. I'm going to read the creation story from Genesis 1. As I read your group's passage, act out how you see that scene taking place. For example, the first group might huddle over someone and then have that person burst out of the huddle to represent the beginning of light. Be creative. You can use any objects in the room as props.**

Allow time for kids to decide how to act out their passage. Then read aloud Genesis 1, pausing after each section to allow groups to act out their passage. Praise kids' efforts. Then ask:

● **What do you notice about the creation process?** (It happened in a logical order; it seemed fast.)

● **What do you think the writer of Genesis 1 wanted us to know about God and our world?** (God is the loving creator of all that is; everything originated from God.)

Say: **Now let's read further. Genesis 2 tells the same story but in a different way.**

Assign volunteers to read aloud different parts of Genesis 2:4-25. Then ask:

● **What's different about the two stories?** (They seem to contradict each other; the emphasis is on different things.)

● **Which one do you like better? Explain.** (The first one, because it seemed more ordered; the second one, because it talked more about humanity.)

3 Branching Out—(For each person, you'll need a pencil and a photocopy of the "Creation Themes" handout on page 43.)

Say: **Let's look for some of the significance in these two stories.**

Give kids each a pencil and a "Creation Themes" handout. Form groups of three or fewer.

Say: **Read each scripture on the handout, and write on the tree what you think is the most important point in that scripture.**

Bring everyone together and discuss each of the scriptures. Here are possible themes:

● Genesis 1:1—God is the creator.
● Genesis 1:4, 10, 12, 18, 21, 25, 31—God created all things good.
● Genesis 1:27—We were created in God's image.
● Genesis 1:29-30—God made us caretakers of creation.
● Genesis 2:16-17—God gave us freedom with limits.

Ask:

● **How do you feel knowing you're created in God's image?** (I feel special; I feel responsible to do what's right.)

● **Why do you think it's important to know that God created everything good?** (We need to see that bad things came because of people; we need to see that God's nature is good.)

● **What does it mean that God gives us freedom within limits?** (God gives us everything we need, not everything we want; God gives us limits to protect us.)

● **How should we take care of creation?** (Keep it clean; preserve endangered species.)

Say: **Taking care of the Earth is an important issue. Many people wonder how long we can stay alive on this planet. Let's explore how well people have done at taking care of the Earth.**

4 **Globe Connections**—(You'll need a beach ball with a globe pattern on it. For each person, you'll need a 6-foot piece of yarn, tape, a 3×5 card and a pencil.)

Inflate the globe. Give kids each a 6-foot piece of yarn and a piece of tape. Have kids each tie their yarn to their wrist and tape the other end of the yarn to the globe.

Give each person a 3×5 card, a pencil and a piece of tape. Say: **We've damaged the Earth in significant ways. We were told to take care of it, but we've abused that privilege. On your card write one thing we've done to hurt the Earth.**

For example, kids might write "polluted streams" or "burned forests." As kids finish, have them each tape their card to the globe (kids should still be taped to the globe).

When everyone is finished, have kids each share what they wrote. As they share, let the air out of the globe. Then ask:

● **How does it feel to be tied to the deflated earth?** (It feels sad; I feel angry about all we've done.)

● **In what ways is polluting the world like letting the air out of this globe?** (It makes the Earth look bad; it takes away the Earth's purpose.)

Have kids each retrieve their card from the globe. On the other side of the card, have them each write one thing they can do to keep the Earth clean and good—as God intended.

For example, one person might say, "I could recycle grocery bags from the store" or "I could plant a tree." As each person shares, blow a little air into the globe until it's reinflated. Remove the yarn from the globe, and set the globe aside.

5 **Creation Celebration**—(You'll need tape, newsprint, a marker and a Bible.)

Tape a sheet of newsprint to each wall. Label the newsprint sheets "God," "Self," "Others" and "Nature," respectively. Form four groups, and have groups each stand next to a different sign. Give each group a marker.

Say: **These four signs represent four areas in our lives God wants us to celebrate and enjoy. Look at your sign. Think about a specific way you can celebrate that area of your life. For example, someone in the "God" group might write, "I can worship God with my guitar." Someone in the**

"Others" group might write, "I can go for a walk with a special friend." Write your response on the sign, then explain it to your group.

When everyone is finished, gather everyone in a circle and have volunteers each repeat what they shared in their group. Then say: **God has given us many things to enjoy and take care of. As we close, let's praise God for the freedoms and responsibilities he's given.**

Set the globe from activity 4 in the center of the circle. Read Psalm 8 responsively together as a closing prayer.

by Mike Gillespie

Creation Themes

Write the main points in each of these scriptures in the tree near the appropriate Bible reference.

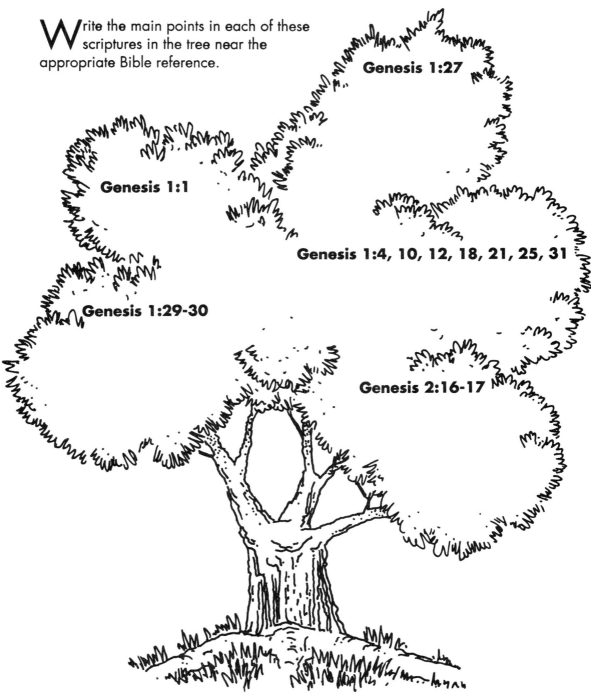

Genesis 1:27

Genesis 1:1

Genesis 1:4, 10, 12, 18, 21, 25, 31

Genesis 1:29-30

Genesis 2:16-17

The Human Journey

Life is a journey. Throughout the journey, all of us experience similar events: our bodies grow; wrinkles begin at 12 years old; nervous systems finish development around 25; and daily food and liquid keep us alive.

But beyond the physical journey through life, there's also a spiritual journey. For the Christian that journey begins and ends with God. Through faith in Jesus Christ we gain the promise of abundant life now and eternal life later.

Use this meeting to help kids understand the nature of humanity in a fallen world and see how Christ's death and Resurrection can set us free.

Objectives

In this meeting kids will:
- evaluate their value as beings created in God's image;
- see how sin severed people's relationships with God;
- discover why they can't reach God on their own;
- understand God's forgiveness through Jesus Christ; and
- learn about God's promises for life today and in the future.

THE MEETING

1 **Getting to Know Me**—(For each person, you'll need construction paper, a marker, scissors and a safety pin. Photocopy and cut apart the "Footprint Steps" on pages 50 through 52. Tape the footprints in numerical order to the walls of your meeting room.)

As kids arrive, have them each make a name tag, following the instructions on footprint #1. Provide construction paper, markers and scissors. Encourage kids to ask each other for positive descriptive words about themselves. Have kids each pin their name tag to their clothing. Allow kids to read each other's name tags.

After a few minutes, call everyone together and say: **Life is a journey. It involves numerous events along the way. Like the physical journey of life, there's also a spiritual journey. Today we'll travel along a spiritual route to see what's involved in the spiritual side of being human.**

Have a volunteer read aloud footprint #2. Have kids each respond.

Say: **Your feelings about your lives can change from day to day—even the way you feel about yourself. But God sees the truth about who we are all the time.**

2 **The Good News**—(You'll need a large mirror with a "You are made in the image of God" sign attached to the front of it. Turn the mirror toward the wall. For each person, you'll need a photocopy of the "Made in God's Image" handout on page 53, a Bible and a pencil.)

Read aloud the instructions on footprint #3, and have a volunteer do what it says. Have kids each look at their image in the mirror. Then ask:

● **What does it mean to be made in God's image?** (It means we're like him in some ways; it means he used himself as a model when he made us.)

Say: **Let's look at the characteristics in people that are similar to God's characteristics.**

Give kids each a "Made in God's Image" handout, a Bible and a pencil. Designate each corner of the room as a different letter: A, B, C or D. Designate the center of the room as E. Read aloud the first scripture, and allow 10 seconds for kids to decide which answer from the list on the right is correct. Then have kids each run to the part of the room that corresponds to their answer. After everyone has chosen an answer, give the correct answer. Then repeat the procedure for the next scripture.

When everyone is finished, go over the answers and discuss kids' responses. The correct answers are 1. d; 2. c; 3. e; 4. b; 5. a.

After the activity, say: **You're important to God. He made you like him.**

Proceed to footprint #4, asking kids to respond to each question.

3 The Bad News—(You'll need several newspapers, a large garbage bag and eight inflated balloons, each with one of the "Missing the Mark" scriptures from page 54 inside. You'll also need a trash can or bucket. For each person, you'll need a Bible. Use a marker to write, "Psalm 53:1-3" on a newspaper.)

Say: **Although you're very different from those around you, there's something all humans share in common.**

Hold up the newspaper with Psalm 53:1-3 written on it. Have a volunteer read aloud Psalm 53:1-3 from a Bible as the others listen for what the verses say about the condition of people today. Ask:

● **Do you agree with the Psalmist's point of view? Why or why not?**

● **How do corruption and injustice keep people from a relationship with God?** (Corrupt people don't care about God; some people never hear about God, so they're kept from him.)

Read aloud footprint #5, and do what it says. Give each team several newspapers. Tell teams they have three minutes to find the most examples of sin and corruption in the newspapers. Instruct kids to tear out headlines, pictures, stories, advertising and other items related to sin.

After three minutes call on each team to share its "sins." Say: **Now we need to clean up our mess.**

Pass around the garbage bag. Have kids each wad up all the newspapers as quickly as possible. Then say: **Look how dirty your hands are!**

Ask:

● **If you identified sins in the newspapers, what could the black ink that's left on your hands stand for?** (Guilt; results of sin.)

Don't allow kids to wash their hands. Read aloud footprint #6, letting kids brainstorm responses to the questions.

Go to footprint #7 and say: **At footprint #7 we'll see how sin is like an arrow that misses the mark.**

Read aloud footprint #7.

Have a volunteer read aloud Romans 3:23. Have kids brainstorm a definition for sin.

After you've guided kids toward a good definition, illustrate Romans 3:23 by having kids each attempt to shoot a balloon into a trash can or bucket. Set the "firing line" about 5 feet from the bucket or trash can. Have kids each try to toss a balloon into the bucket. After everyone has tried, ask:

● **How is missing the trash can like being human?** (We want to live a good life, but we miss the goal; we want to love God, but we fall short on our own.)

For ideas on how to hit the target, have kids pop the balloons and look up the Bible verses inside. Have kids each read their passage. Then ask:

● **What do these verses say about "missing the mark"?** (Everyone falls short of God's ideal; God is willing to forgive us when we do wrong.)

Read aloud footprint #8, allowing kids to respond to each question.

 The Best News—(You'll need a damp towel, a wadded-up newspaper and a bowl of dirt. For each person, you'll need a flimsy paper plate, two pieces of yarn and a marker.)

Say: **We see now that no one can overcome sin by acting religious or by living a strict life.**

Have a volunteer read aloud footprint #9. Then say: **God loves you enough to create a way for you to renew fellowship with him. That renewal is through Jesus Christ.**

Read aloud John 3:16. Say: **God has made a way for you, but you have a choice. I'll set three items on the table. You'll each have a chance to choose an item with which you can wash away your sins (the black on your hands). But first, let's look more closely at the sin in our lives.**

Give kids each a flimsy paper plate, two pieces of yarn and a marker. Say: **On your plate write a sin you recognize in your life. No one will see this. Punch holes in opposite sides of**

your plate, tie strings in the holes and tie the plate onto your face with the sin facing toward your face.

Be sure kids can't see around their "masks."

Set out the damp towel, the wadded-up newspaper and a bowl of dirt. Number the items (kids won't know which number refers to which item). Then have kids come to the table one at a time and say by number which item they want to try to wash off the black ink with. Tell everyone to be silent during this activity.

After everyone has had a turn, have kids each remove their mask and see the results. Ask:

● **Why was it hard to make a good choice?** (Because the mask kept me from seeing; because I didn't have any guidance.)

● **How are your masks like sin in your life?** (They keep me from seeing God's will for me; they make it hard to know where I'm going.)

Say: **To come to God you have to be willing to put sin away. You did that by removing your mask. God removes your mask when you ask for his forgiveness.**

Let kids wipe their hands with the damp towel as you read aloud 1 John 1:9.

Read aloud footprint #10, allowing kids to respond to each question.

5 **Who, Me?**—(You'll need a photocopy of "Footprints" on page 54. For each person, you'll need a Bible, a pencil, a sheet of paper and a piece of tape.)

Say: **Not only does God remove the guilt of sin from our lives, he also promises to help us be more like him.**

Read aloud Matthew 5:3-12. Have a volunteer read aloud footprint #11, and have kids each follow the instructions. Give kids each a pencil, and allow time for kids each to write on the back of their name tag. Call on volunteers to share their new name tags. Encourage kids each to place their name tag in a place where they can see the promises daily.

Read aloud the final footprint and "Footprints." Ask:

● **How does this parable help you understand humanity's relationship to God?** (We're his children; he sees us through hard times.)

● **How has this meeting changed your perspective on your relationship with God?** (I realize that God wants to be with me; I want to work harder to make the right choices in life.)

Give kids each a sheet of paper and a piece of tape. Have them each tape their paper to their name tag. Say: **For our closing, let's recognize how God has helped each of us become more like him. On each person's sheet, write one way you see Jesus' character in him or her.**

When everyone is finished, allow kids to read their name tags. Then close with prayer, thanking God for helping us become more like him each day.

by Ann Cannon

Footprint Steps

Photocopy and cut apart these footprints, and tape them to your meeting room walls.

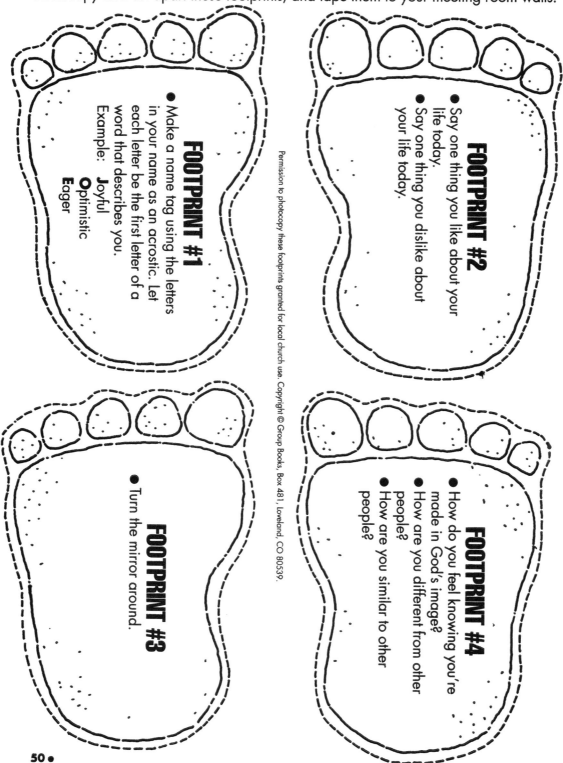

FOOTPRINT #1

- Make a name tag using the letters in your name as an acrostic. Let each letter be the first letter of a word that describes you.

Example: **J**oyful
Optimistic
Eager

FOOTPRINT #2

- Say one thing you like about your life today.
- Say one thing you dislike about your life today.

FOOTPRINT #3

- Turn the mirror around.

FOOTPRINT #4

- How do you feel knowing you're made in God's image?
- How are you different from other people?
- How are you similar to other people?

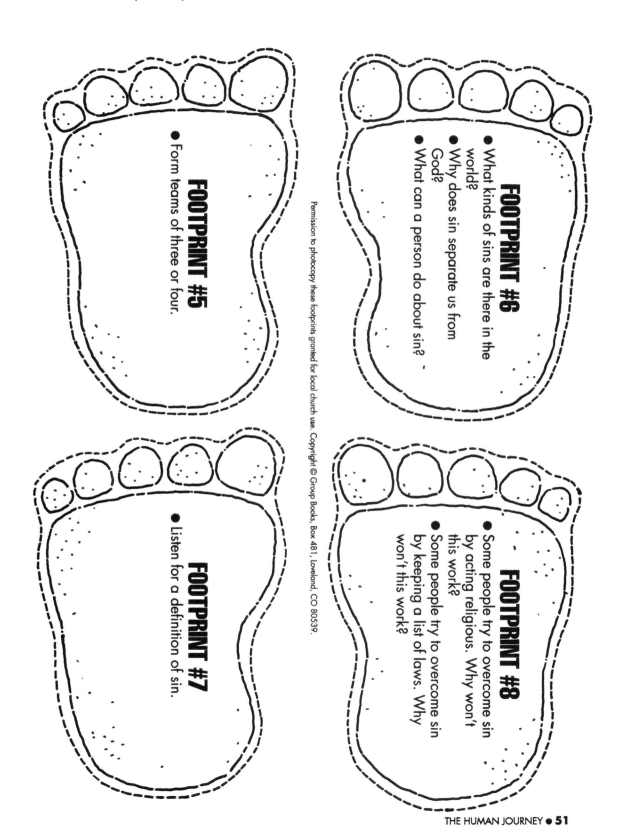

FOOTPRINT #5

● Form teams of three or four.

FOOTPRINT #6

● What kinds of sins are there in the world?
● Why does sin separate us from God?
● What can a person do about sin?

FOOTPRINT #7

● Listen for a definition of sin.

FOOTPRINT #8

● Some people try to overcome sin by acting religious. Why won't this work?
● Some people try to overcome sin by keeping a list of laws. Why won't this work?

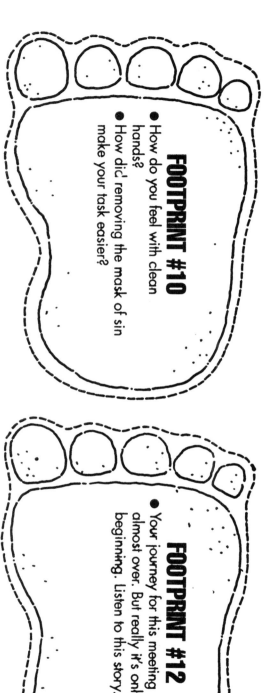

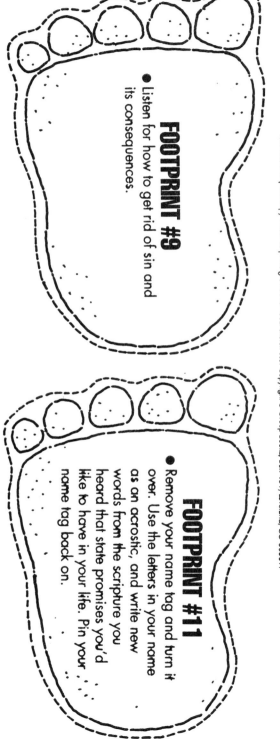

FOOTPRINT #9

- Listen for how to get rid of sin and its consequences.

FOOTPRINT #10

- How do you feel with clean hands?
- How did removing the mask of sin make your task easier?

FOOTPRINT #11

- Remove your name tag and turn it over. Use the letters in your name as an acrostic, and write new words from the scripture you heard that state promises you'd like to have in your life. Pin your name tag back on.

FOOTPRINT #12

- Your journey for this meeting is almost over. But really it's only beginning. Listen to this story.

made in God's Image

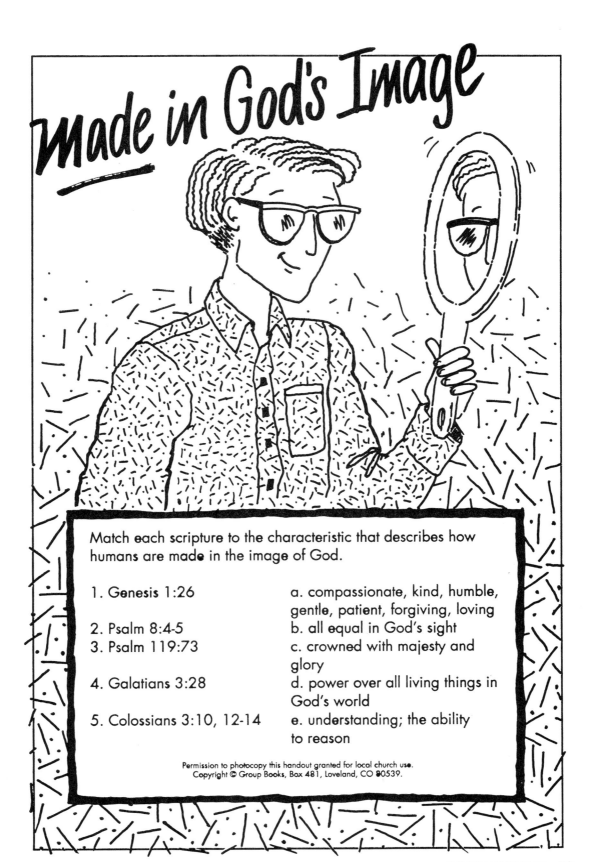

Match each scripture to the characteristic that describes how humans are made in the image of God.

1. Genesis 1:26

2. Psalm 8:4-5
3. Psalm 119:73

4. Galatians 3:28

5. Colossians 3:10, 12-14

a. compassionate, kind, humble, gentle, patient, forgiving, loving
b. all equal in God's sight
c. crowned with majesty and glory
d. power over all living things in God's world
e. understanding; the ability to reason

Footprints

One night a man had a dream. He dreamed he was walking along the beach with the Lord. Across the sky flashed scenes from his life. For each scene, he noticed two sets of footprints in the sand; one belonging to him, and the other to the Lord.

When the last scene of his life flashed before him, he looked back at the footprints in the sand. He noticed that many times along the path of his life there was only one set of footprints. He also noticed that it happened at the very lowest and saddest times in his life.

This really bothered him and he questioned the Lord about it. "Lord, you said that once I decided to follow you, you'd walk with me all the way. But I have noticed that during the most troublesome times in my life, there is only one set of footprints. I don't understand why when I needed you most you would leave me."

The Lord replied, "My precious, precious child, I love you and I would never leave you. During your times of trial and suffering, when you see only one set of footprints, it was then that I carried you."

Author Unknown

Missing the Mark

Photocopy and cut apart these verses, then place each in a separate balloon.

Psalm 51:3-4	Romans 7:19
Mark 14:38	Romans 7:22-23
Romans 7:15	Romans 7:25
Romans 7:18	1 John 1:8-9

Life isn't fair. A teenager who follows God gets killed by a drunk driver. The drunk teenager who hit him comes out of it without a scratch. Good kids can face rough times. And bad kids can seem to sail through life without a care. Getting a proper perspective on evil in the world can get confusing. But the Bible presents God's perspective on sin, evil and suffering that Christians—especially young people—need to understand.

Use this meeting to help kids understand why sin, evil and suffering exist in the world.

Objectives

In this meeting kids will:

- list good and bad things that happen to people;
- explore how people in the Bible responded to sin, evil and suffering;
- learn why it's better to live God's way; and
- affirm each other for helping them trust God—even in hard times.

THE MEETING

1 **Ordering Events**—(You'll need paper, pencils, newsprint, markers and tape.)

Form two groups, and give them each a sheet of paper and a pencil. Have one group list 10 bad things that've happened in the last month. Have the other group list 10 good things that've happened in the last month. Allow three minutes for groups to make their lists.

Call time, then have groups each rank their lists from one to 10 (1=worst or best; 10=least worst or least best). Give groups each a sheet of newsprint and a marker, and have them each write their list in order on newsprint and tape it to the wall. Then have groups each explain their list, telling why they ranked the events as they did.

Say: **Life isn't fair. Bad things happen to good people; good things happen to bad people. Getting a proper perspective on evil in the world can get confusing. But the Bible presents a distinctive perspective on sin, evil and suffering that Christians need to understand.**

2 **"Job" Descriptions**—(For each person, you'll need a photocopy of the "Glance at Job" handout on page 59 and a Bible.)

Give each kid a "Glance at Job" handout and a Bible. Read aloud the opening statement on the handout. Form groups of four. Have groups each review the scriptures listed on the handout and develop a brief skit that illustrates the four major acts.

When groups are ready, have them each present their skit. Praise each group's efforts, and comment on how each skit parallels Job's story.

After all groups have presented their skits, ask:

● **How'd you feel as you acted out Job's story?** (It made me feel nervous; it made me wonder about God.)

● **How is Job's story like your own?** (Sometimes bad things happen and I don't know why; sometimes I feel like God is against me.)

● **Why did God allow bad things to happen to Job?** (To test his heart; to make him a better person.)

● **Why does God sometimes allow bad things to happen to us?** (To prepare us for harder times ahead; to make us appreciate God's grace.)

Say: **Like Job, we need to listen to God, recognize his justice, repent of our sin and accept God as Creator, sustainer and guide of our lives.**

Headline News—(You'll need tape, a sheet of newsprint, five markers and five Bibles.)

Read aloud Matthew 5:45b. Say: **Good and bad happen to everyone. But life with God promises certain good things that can't come any other way. And a life without God means certain bad things are inevitable.**

Form five groups. A group can be one person. Tape a sheet of newsprint to the wall, and draw a line down the middle of it. Write on one side, "Life With God." Write on the other side, "Life Without God." Give groups each a marker and a Bible. Assign each group one of these Bible passages:

● Ephesians 2:1-10;
● Ephesians 4:17-32;
● Ephesians 5:1-20;
● Colossians 2:6-17; and
● Colossians 3:5-17.

Have groups each read their Bible passage. Then have groups pull examples from the scripture of "Life With God" or "Life Without God" and write them on the newsprint under the appropriate heading. For example, under "Life With God," kids might write, "made alive in Christ." Under "Life Without God," kids might write, "dead in sin."

When groups are finished, have them each explain what they wrote on the newsprint and how it applies to their lives. Ask:

● **What can you gain by living your life with God?** (You have God's peace; God makes you righteous.)

● **What's the price for living life without God?** (You'll be alone; you'll have no purpose in life.)

● **Why doesn't God always keep bad things from happening to Christians?** (Because we need things to help shape our character; because we need to sympathize with others who go through the same bad experiences.)

Then say: **It's true that bad things happen to good people.**

But God gives us the resources—the mind of Christ, fellowship with other Christians and the truth from God's Word—to help us deal with life's experiences. It's only as we choose to live in relationship to God that these resources are made available to us.

4 **Cloud Cheers**—(You'll need a Bible. For each person, you'll need a pencil and a piece of tape.)

Say: **Back in the story of Job, we saw how Job never really discovered God's reasons for allowing bad things to happen to him. In the same way, some bad things that happen to us will never be explained until we get to heaven. But many Christians have gone before us, leaving us an example to persevere even when we don't know all the answers.**

Read aloud Hebrews 12:1-2. Give each kid a pencil and a piece of tape, and have them each draw a cloud on the back of one of their handouts. Have kids each tape their cloud to their back. Inside each person's cloud, have kids each list how that person helps them trust God—even in hard times. When kids are finished, let them read their clouds.

Close with the following prayer. Have kids repeat each line after you.

Thank you, God, for my cloud of witnesses.
Help me move away from sin.
Keep me running toward the goal you've set for me.
And allow us to support each other along the way. Amen.

by Arlo Reichter

Glance at Job

Job's story in the Old Testament provides a classic example of bad things happening to good people. Job's friends believed God always rewards good and punishes bad, so when bad things happened to Job and his family, his friends assumed Job had sinned. Although sin hadn't caused his suffering, Job did become arrogant in the midst of suffering and evil. He eventually recognized his sin and repented.

In your group, create a contemporary play containing four major acts similar to the four acts of Job. You can use any characters, time in history or settings you want. But your skit must illustrate the points made in Job's story. The four major acts in Job's story are:

I. Job's Arrogance (Job 29:1-25)
II. Job Listens to God (Job 33:1-14)
III. God Is Just (Job 36:22-26)
IV. Job Repents (Job 42:1-6)

The Family of Faith

A faith commitment is more than a one-time, fire-insurance experience. It's a transformation, a lifestyle, a family adoption. When a person believes in Christ, he or she relates to God as a parent and other Christians as brothers and sisters—like a family. As in all families, there are times of joy and heartache, confusion and reaffirmation, growth and regression. Most of all, there's the security of always belonging to God, always being loved by God and always being understood by God. These assurances give Christians the foundation for growth and maturity.

Faith is a journey—a process. It begins with trusting Christ as Savior and Lord and continues through life on Earth. This session studies Christian faith in three stages—realizing that each stage is closely related to the other, and none can be clearly delineated. These stages are:

- placing faith in Christ,
- increasing in Christlikeness, and
- enjoying Christ in heaven.

Use this meeting to help kids understand their faith as a growing relationship with God that culminates in heaven.

Objectives

In this meeting kids will:

- notice how and why Christians are different;
- distinguish between joy based on circumstances and joy based on a relationship with God;
- see faith from Christ's perspective;
- draw images of heaven; and
- affirm their need for faith in Christ.

THE MEETING

1 A Christian I Know—(You'll need a ball of yarn.)

Have kids form a circle. Hold up a ball of yarn, and explain that everyone will tell about a Christian they know and how that person's life is different from someone who isn't a Christian. You start. After you talk about a Christian, toss the ball of yarn to someone else in the circle, but hold onto the end so a string of yarn stretches between you and that person. Have that person share next, then have him or her hold onto the end of the yarn and toss the yarn to a third person. Continue until everyone has held the yarn and a web of yarn has been created in the circle. Then ask:

● **What's the distinguishing characteristic of Christians?** (They've accepted Jesus; they love each other.)

Say: **The beginning of Christian faith is as simple as trusting Jesus as Savior and Lord. Living out faith can be as intriguing and as complex as the web we've created with our yarn. During this session we'll study some of these complexities, mysteries and joys.**

2 A New Life—(For each person, you'll need a piece of yarn and a Bible.)

Cut foot-long strips of yarn from the yarn web. Give one to each person. Then say: **On the floor, "draw" your piece of yarn to represent "joy."**

When kids are finished, have them each explain their shape. Note that some shapes emphasize joy from an event, while others emphasize joy from relationships. Discuss the difference between happiness based on circumstances and happiness based on a relationship with Christ.

Say: **Faith in Christ brings the deepest and longest-lasting joy possible. That joy persists no matter what the circumstances. It gives a sense of well-being and the assurance of knowing that no matter what happens, God will take care of you. This joy comes through being united with Jesus Christ. He makes you the happiest you can be.**

Say: **During this meeting we'll focus on one Bible book to learn three basic truths about our faith commitment. This** book is Philippians and its theme is joy in Christ.

If needed, show kids where to find Philippians in their Bibles. Then say: **The three truths we'll study spell BIG—**
- **Begin trusting Christ;**
- **Increase in Christlikeness; and**
- **Go to heaven.**

At some point we *begin* our faith relationship with Christ. Then while we live on Earth we *increase* in Christlikeness. After death we *go* to heaven where we live forever in the presence of God and other Christians.

Trading Steps—(You'll need a Bible, a sheet of newsprint and a marker.)

Ask:
- **When does Christianity start in a person's life?** (When you're very young, praying beside your bed at night; when you decide to turn your life over to Christ.)

Read aloud Philippians 1:6. On a sheet of newsprint, write the words: "need," "love," "accept" and "relationship." Circle the words as you explain what they mean. Say: **Becoming a Christian begins by understanding your *need* for God. Only he can meet your need for belonging and love. Then you recognize that God *loves* you even though you don't deserve it. Finally, becoming a Christian begins by *accepting* God's love in the person Jesus Christ. A faith commitment is a *relationship* rather than a set of rules or a religion. Like any love relationship, it grows and deepens as you learn more about how to please God.**

Now write these words and phrases: "good deeds," "religiousness," and "acknowledging God's existence." Then ask:
- **How do these things represent what a faith commitment is not?** (You aren't a Christian just because you go to church; being a good person doesn't make you a Christian.)
- **Why don't these actions make you a Christian?** (Christianity depends on knowing God, not doing good things; God looks at your heart, not just your actions.)

A New View—(You'll need a Bible. For each person, you'll need a piece of blue- or rose-color plastic wrap, a photocopy of the "Eyes of Christ" handout on page 67 and a pair of scissors.)

Give kids each a piece of blue- or rose-color plastic wrap, and have them each look through their plastic wrap. Ask:

● **How does the world look different?** (Everything looks pale; those flowers look so much brighter.)

● **What do you see that you wouldn't see without these "glasses"?**

Say: **Our faith relationship is a process of becoming more and more like Jesus Christ. Part of this process is seeing yourself, relationships and the world in a different light.**

Read aloud Philippians 2:1-18. Give kids each an "Eyes of Christ" handout and a pair of scissors. Have kids make their glasses and put them on. Then ask:

● **How would seeing through Christ's eyes affect your relationships?** (I'd love everyone the same; I'd see something valuable in each person.)

● **How would seeing through Christ's eyes affect your faith?** (I'd know that God was in control, no matter what; I'd trust God more.)

● **How would you see circumstances differently?** (I wouldn't worry as much; I'd try harder to take advantage of opportunities that come along.)

● **How would seeing through Christ's eyes affect your actions?** (I wouldn't waste as much time; I'd spend more time doing things for others.)

 Rolling Applications—(You'll need a Bible. You'll also need photocopies of the "Philippians Cube" on page 68 and the "Experience Cube" on page 69. Assemble the cubes before the activity.)

Say: **Living your faith is a step-by-step, day-to-day process. It means looking at things the way God sees them and responding the way God would respond.**

Invite a volunteer to read aloud Philippians 3:10-16. Hold up the "Philippians Cube," and point out that six phrases from Philippians 3:10-14 are printed on the sides of this cube. Hold up the "Experience

Cube," and explain that these are experiences we face daily. Say: **Each of you will roll both cubes and name a way to live your faith by expressing the Bible truth you roll in the experience you roll. For example, if you roll "to know Christ" and "how I spend my free time" you might say, "I'll choose music that encourages me to understand and live like Jesus rather than music that confuses or contradicts my relationship with Jesus."**

After everyone has had a turn, ask:

● **How does living like Jesus bring joy?** (Because you know he loves you; because he's joyful.)

● **Why does obeying him bring freedom?** (Because he knows what's best for you; because when you give him control, you don't have to worry about things anymore.)

6 Forever Results—(You'll need tape and a large sheet of newsprint. For each of five teams, you'll need a Bible and a marker.)

Say: **Christians on Earth are far from perfect, and conditions on Earth are far from perfect. But there is a place where there are perfect conditions and all the people are perfect.**

Ask:

● **What is that place called?** (Heaven.)

Read aloud Philippians 3:20-21. Explain that heaven is our home—our final destination—and when Jesus Christ returns to Earth, or when we die, we'll go there. Ask:

● **How does knowing this affect how you feel about life?** (It puts me at ease; it gives me something to look forward to.)

Say: **Describing heaven is difficult because it's so different from anything we've ever experienced. It's like describing color to a blind person or describing adulthood to an infant. Philippians tells us briefly about heaven, but Revelation 21 gives us images of heaven that help us understand just what heaven will be like.**

Tape a large sheet of newsprint to the wall. Form five teams, and give each team a Bible and a marker. A team can be one person. Assign each team one of the following portions of Revelation 21:

● Revelation 21:1-4;

● Revelation 21:5-7;

- Revelation 21:9-14;
- Revelation 21:15-21; and
- Revelation 21:22-27.

Have teams each draw on the newsprint a picture that represents their passage.

Compliment each team's drawing, and point out how it expresses scripture. Ask each person:

- **Which is your favorite image of heaven and why?**
- **How does this image affect your life now?**

Read aloud Revelation 21:8. Say: **Not everyone goes to heaven. Some choose to go to hell by rejecting God and a relationship with him.** Ask:

- **Why would people choose to stay separated from God?** (Because they want to control their own lives; because they don't believe God wants the best for them.)

- **How does hell begin the moment you reject God?** (Life is harder without God; people without God have no hope for a future after they die.)

- **How does heaven begin the moment you put your faith in Christ?** (God is with you all the time; God gives you joy and peace from heaven.)

7 Freed From and To—(You'll need a sheet of newsprint and several markers.)

Ask:

- **What are the three truths we've studied?** (Beginning our faith, increasing in Christlikeness and going to heaven where we live forever in the presence of God.)

- **How do these steps lead to freedom?** (We become free from sin; we become free to follow God fully.)

On a sheet of newsprint, write these two headings: "Freed From ... " and "Freed To ... "

Provide markers for volunteers to write completions for each list. Possibilities include:

Freed From ...
- loneliness.
- confusion.
- powerlessness.
- meaninglessness.
- many problems.

Freed To ...
- belong to God's family.
- have God help me understand.
- receive God's power.
- have a purpose.
- live God's way.

Ask:

● **Which is your favorite "Freed From ... Freed To" completion?**

● **Why do (or would) you want to be freed?**

● **What other word would you use to define freed?**

Encourage words such as "completed," "saved" and "rescued" and youth-created words such as "happy-fied."

8 Why I Need Jesus—(You'll need a Bible. For each person, you'll need a 3×5 card and a pencil.)

Ask:

● **Why do we need to trust in Jesus?** (Because we can't get to heaven on our own; because we've sinned.)

Say: **Without God we're incomplete. As a philosopher has said, there is a God-shaped emptiness in each of us and only God can fill it.**

Read aloud the promises in Philippians 4:13 and 4:19. Give each kid a 3×5 card and a pencil. Have them each write responses on their card to these questions:

● **Which is your favorite promise?**

● **How will it impact the way you live your faith?**

Have kids form a circle. Invite kids each to talk with God about their relationship with him. Suggest they start their prayers with "God, I'm glad you ... " or "I want to show I love you by ... "

Close by reading aloud Philippians 4:13 and 4:19 again.

by Karen Dockrey

EYES OF CHRIST

CUT OUT

CUT OUT

CUT

Cut apart these glasses, fold as marked and hold them to your eyes.

FOLD   FOLD

PHILIPPIANS CUBE

Photocopy, cut apart and assemble this cube.

fold under

PHILIPPIANS CUBE

Let us live up to what we have already attained.

PHILIPPIANS CUBE

PHILIPPIANS CUBE

PHILIPPIANS CUBE

fold under

fold under

PHILIPPIANS CUBE

Forgetting what is behind and straining toward what is ahead.

PHILIPPIANS CUBE

PHILIPPIANS CUBE

PHILIPPIANS CUBE

fold under

PHILIPPIANS CUBE

To know Christ.

PHILIPPIANS CUBE

PHILIPPIANS CUBE

PHILIPPIANS CUBE

PHILIPPIANS CUBE

Press on toward the goal to win the prize for which God has called me.

PHILIPPIANS CUBE

PHILIPPIANS CUBE

fold under

fold under

fold under

PHILIPPIANS CUBE

Becoming like him in his death, and so somehow, to attain to the resurrection from the dead.

PHILIPPIANS CUBE

PHILIPPIANS CUBE

PHILIPPIANS CUBE

PHILIPPIANS CUBE

I press on to take hold of that for which Christ Jesus took hold of me.

PHILIPPIANS CUBE

PHILIPPIANS CUBE

PHILIPPIANS CUBE

EXPERIENCE CUBE

Photocopy, cut apart and assemble this cube.

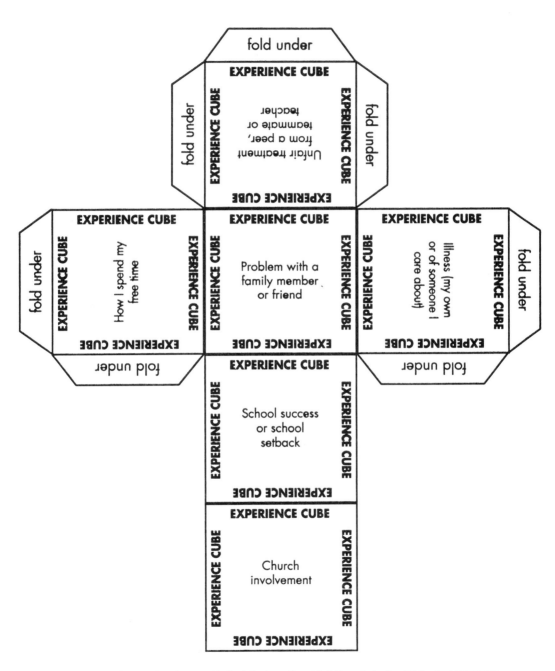

Why the Church?

"**W**hy should I go to church? It's just a bunch of old people who frown at me because of my hair!"

"I just don't fit in there. And I'm sick of boring sermons."

"I only have one day of the week to sleep in! Give me a break!"

These comments are typical of many teenagers when church is mentioned. According to one study, almost 50 percent of kids never or rarely attend church.

But the church has so much to offer kids today:

● a place to belong where kids won't be ridiculed or drawn into dangerous activities;

● a place where they can learn about God and grow in faith; and

● a place where they each can begin to take their place and serve God as part of Christ's body.

And kids need all those things.

Use this meeting to help your kids see what the church can really mean to them.

Objectives

In this meeting kids will:

● sort out truths and misconceptions about the church;

● examine what the Bible says about the church;

● experience working together with each person contributing;

● demonstrate how we need each other; and

● celebrate being part of the church.

THE MEETING

1 **What's the Church Anyway?**—(For each group of three or four, you'll need tape and a photocopy of the "Is It or Isn't It?" handout on page 74. Cut apart the phrases, making a set for each group. On a chalkboard or newsprint, write the headings "The Church Is . . ." and "The Church Isn't . . ." each at the top of a column.)

Form groups of three or four. Say: **Today we're going to take a look at the church. First let's have some fun with what we know about it. I'm going to give each group a set of phrases that complete one of the two headings: "The Church Is . . ." or "The Church Isn't . . ."**

On "go," decide where the phrases fit. Then tape them under the proper heading. If you're right, you win. If not, take them back to your group and try again.

Give each group tape and a set of phrases from the "Is It or Isn't It?" handout. Then start the game.

The way the phrases are listed on the handout is correct. When a group gets them all correct, declare the winner. Then go over each phrase, discussing why it does or doesn't describe the church.

2 **Why Church?**—(You'll need Bibles, pencils and paper.)
If you have fewer than 12 kids, do this activity as a single group, having the group work with all three of the scripture passages. If you have more kids, form three groups and assign one of these passages to each group: Matthew 28:18-20; Acts 2:42-47; and Ephesians 4:11-16.

Form a circle. Give groups each a sheet of paper and a pencil. Say: **Imagine your group is a college creative-writing class. The professor has given you this assignment: Read the scripture you've been given. Then as a group write a brief essay discussing the church, based on that scripture.**

Your essay must be as many sentences long as there are people in your group, and each person must write one sentence. You may discuss what to cover in your essay and help one another decide what to write. Begin with the person with the most red on, and go around your group.

Have kids each read aloud their sentence as they write.

When kids are finished, have groups each read their essay aloud. Then ask:

● **What'd you learn about the church from these passages?** (Jesus gave the disciples the command to tell about him; God gives us gifts to help us serve him.)

● **How was writing the essay together like serving God together in the church?** (We had to work together; each person had something to contribute.)

● **What does it mean to be part of "the body of Christ"?** (To be part of his church; to work together in the church like parts of a body work together.)

● **From these passages, why would you say God established the church?** (To let others know about him; to give Christians others who care about them.)

So What's It to Me?—(You'll need an old paperback book at least ¾ inch thick.)

Say: **We've talked about what the church is and why God started it, but now it's time to take a look at what that means to us.**

Pass around the paperback book, and challenge kids to tear it in half while keeping it shut tight. Allow five seconds for kids each to attempt to rip the book in half.

When all kids have tried and failed, open the book and tear it apart, giving kids each a 20- to 30-page section. Then have kids each tear their section in half. Ask:

● **How is this book like the church?** (It's tough to tear it apart when it's all together; without all the parts it's not a complete story.)

● **How are the small sections of the book like individual Christians?** (It's a lot easier to destroy them when they're separated; they each have only part of the story line.)

● **When you face tough times, who do you prefer to have around you—close friends or strangers? Explain.** (Close friends, they'd be more support; strangers, I wouldn't want my friends to see me mess up.)

Say: **In the church we can pull together and help keep any of us from being torn apart. Christians truly are family members on the same side. They're available to help us when we need them. And we can be there to help them too.**

4 **A Place for Me?**—(You'll need 3×5 cards and pencils.)
Pass out 3×5 cards and pencils to all the kids. Say: **Now let's think about how we can take a more active part in the church—by giving and receiving.**

Have kids each write on one side of their card one way they can be a support to someone else in the church. On the other side, have them each write one way they can lean on other people in the church more for help.

When kids are finished, form pairs. Have kids each share with their partner what they wrote on their card. Then have kids each tell their partner one reason they're glad he or she is part of the church. Encourage kids to be sincere and serious in encouraging their partners.

5 **If I Were an Eye?**—(You'll need a Bible, "The Church Isn't . . ." phrases from activity 1, confetti, upbeat Christian music and something to play it on.)
To wrap up the session, read aloud 1 Corinthians 12:12-27. Then say: **In the church, God has given us a place to belong and be needed, a place to learn about him and a place to serve him. And, like Jesus said in Matthew 28:20, he'll be with us always! Let's celebrate what we have together in Christ's church!**

Have kids tear up the "The Church Isn't . . ." phrases. Add confetti, and turn on some upbeat Christian music. Then lead kids in a "Hip, hip, hooray!" cheer for the church, throwing the confetti into the air. Make a game out of it by stuffing confetti down kids' backs or rubbing it in their hair.

After a few minutes, close the meeting with a prayer thanking God for the church.

by Paul Woods

Is It or Isn't It?

Photocopy and cut apart the following phrases, without the headings.

The Church Is . . .

people who make a lot of mistakes while trying to serve God.

a place for hurting people to find comfort and help.

something set up by God to help his people through life.

a group of people sharing common faith and hope in Jesus Christ.

a group of people gifted by God to serve him together.

The Church Isn't . . .

a place for old people to gather and listen to a dull sermon.

a place for good people to meet together and be happy about their goodness.

an old building with stained-glass windows.

a bunch of cranky people who want to keep teenagers from having a good time.

the place where God lives.

Prayer Power!

"**M**ore things are wrought by prayer than this world dreams of. Wherefore, let thy voice rise like a fountain for me night and day." So wrote Alfred, Lord Tennyson (*Idylls of the King: The Passing of Arthur*). But is it true?

Of course! we protest. Why, scripture is full of attestations to the power of prayer! We know people who've been changed by prayer! But for many youth workers, teaching about prayer comes with difficulty because, well, prayer comes with difficulty. Tennyson is interesting, but scripture may be more in tune with our hearts when it says, "Lord, teach us to pray" (Luke 11:1). Prayer is a mystical union with God. It's face-to-face contact with our creator.

Prayer isn't a skill we can teach. But we can guide kids in their understanding of prayer. For example, we can show kids how we pray; we can certainly pray for them; and we can create situations that'll enable them to pray.

Use this meeting to help kids understand prayer and to provide an opportunity for them to grow in prayer.

Objectives

In this meeting kids will:
- explore what's important to them;
- see examples of prayers in the Bible;
- list things they want to talk to God about; and
- compose a group prayer.

THE MEETING

1 **Take It or Leaf It**—(For each person, you'll need a pencil and a photocopy of the "Take It or Leaf It" handout on page 79.)

After everyone is present, give kids each a pencil and a "Take It or Leaf It" handout. Say: **You have a drawing of a simple leaf. As you can see, this leaf—like all others—depends on a complex network of veins to distribute nutrients throughout it. All living things have some sort of system to "keep them going." Let's spend a few minutes talking about what keeps us going.**

Point out that on this leaf, kids can see four or five primary veins. Have kids each write on the veins the four or five most important things in their lives—things that keep them going. For example, someone might write, "music, a good relationship with parents, and the youth group."

When everyone is finished, have kids each share their responses. As kids share, ask them each why they chose the items they did.

2 **Prayer Song**—(For each pair, you'll need a photocopy of the "One Person's Song" handout on page 80 and a pencil.)

Say: **During this meeting, we'll look at something that really keeps me going. In fact, it keeps millions of people all around the world going—prayer. Sometimes it's easy to think Christians are just being silly when they pray—like they're only talking to themselves. But the Bible tells us God hears our prayers and answers them. Let's examine this issue more closely.**

Form pairs, and give each pair a "One Person's Song" handout and a pencil. Say: **This is an actual song written by a person who was dealing with his feelings about God. Please read the song, and then answer the questions with your partner.**

After pairs have discussed the questions, call everyone together and discuss the questions as a group. Ask volunteers to explain why they chose the answers they did. Then say: **The prayer you read comes from Psalm 42 in the Bible. It teaches us that God wants us to pray and be honest about how we feel.**

3 **Prayer Roles**—(You'll need a photocopy of "A Prayer Pair" handout on page 81. Before the meeting, cut apart the handout and assign the parts to two "dramatic" kids in the youth group. Have them be prepared to read their parts during this activity.)

Say: **We're going to look at two more examples of prayer and decide which one we think is more in line with what God wants.**

Introduce the first dramatist, the Religious Person. Have that person act out his or her character with great relish and enthusiasm.

Without pausing to reflect, say: **That's one model. Now let's look at another approach.** Have the second dramatist, the Nerd, act out his or her prayer.

After both dramatists have finished, explain that this skit was based on a passage in the Bible. Have a volunteer read aloud Luke 18:10-14. Then ask:

● **Which of the prayers sounds like it was more acceptable to God? Explain.** (The first one, because that person gave to the church; the second one, because that person was humble.)

● **What was right and what was wrong with these prayers?**

● **What can we learn about prayer from this exercise?** (God isn't fooled by clever words; I can talk to God just as I talk to my friends.)

4 **Prayer Lists**—(You'll need newsprint and a marker, or a chalkboard and chalk. For each person, you'll need a sheet of paper and a pencil.)

On a chalkboard or a sheet of newsprint, number 1 through 10 from top to bottom. Say: **We've talked a lot today about other people talking to God. What about you? If you had the opportunity to talk with God about anything, what would it be? Let's list 10 things we'd like to discuss with God.**

List the suggestions as they come. Some examples might be "Why is there suffering?"; "Why do my parents fight so much?"; or "What do you want me to do with my life?" Don't try to discuss the suggestions, just list them.

When the list is complete, read aloud Philippians 4:6-7. Say:

Thinking about items like those we listed can sometimes make us afraid. But God promises in this scripture that if we ask God to help us and are thankful for what he's doing, then his peace will protect us from fear.

Give kids each a sheet of paper and a pencil. Have kids each write on their paper five concerns they'd like to ask God to help them with and five things they're thankful for. When kids are finished, say: **Take your list home, and tape it to your bathroom mirror. Then pray each morning, asking for God's help in the areas you wrote and thanking him for his work in your life.**

5 **Spinning Thanks**—(No supplies needed.)
Say: **Often when people pray, they fold their hands or perhaps hold hands with each other. As we prepare to leave, we'll pray in a couple of ways. First, we'll thank God for each other.**

Have kids put their arms around each other in a circle. Say: **As we're linked together now, we'll walk around to the left until someone says, "Stop." Then that person will say one thing he or she is thankful for about someone else in the room. For example, someone might say, "I'm thankful for Bob's sense of humor" or "I'm thankful Carol is such a good listener." Then we'll walk to the right until someone else says, "Stop." Each person can only be mentioned once. We'll continue until everyone has been mentioned.**

Note kids who may be "overlooked" in this activity, and affirm them yourself.

6 **Closing Prayers**—(You'll need a sheet of newsprint and a marker, or a chalkboard and chalk. For each person, you'll need a photocopy of the "Seven Tips for Prayer" handout on page 82.)

Have kids stay in the circle with arms linked. Write, "Dear Lord" on a chalkboard or a sheet of newsprint. Say: **Let's take a moment now to talk to God about our time here. I've started the prayer. Let's all finish it. We'll go around the circle and have each person add a phrase to the prayer.** If you have time, have kids each share two or three times.

Allow the group a minute or so to think, and if necessary provide a "jump start" by suggesting words such as "give," "tell" or "show."

After the prayer, give kids each a "Seven Tips for Prayer" handout. Explain that this handout is for kids' personal use, and encourage them to read it carefully at home.

by Dave Carver

Take It or Leaf It

Every leaf—every being—has something that "keeps it going." What keeps you going? What are some things that are important to you? Is it music? sports? friends? your own car?

Think of four or five important things in your life, and write them on the veins of the leaf below.

One Person's Song

Read this song carefully, then answer the questions below. You won't have to share your answers (although you'll have the opportunity), so be honest.

As the deer pants for streams of water, so my soul pants for you, O God. My soul thirsts for God, for the living God. When can I go and meet with God? My tears have been my food day and night, while men say to me all day long, "Where is your God?"

These things I remember as I pour out my soul: how I used to go with the multitude, leading the procession to the house of God, with shouts of joy and thanksgiving among the festive throng.

Why are you downcast, O my soul? Why so disturbed within me? Put your hope in God, for I will yet praise him, my Savior and my God.*

After you read the song, answer these questions:

1. Is this a prayer? Why or why not?

2. At the beginning of the song, how does the person feel about God? What are his emotions?

3. Is there a change in emotions by the end of the song? If so, how can you tell?

4. What's one thing you've felt sad about in your relationship with God?

5. Is it important to pray? Why or why not?

*Scripture taken from Psalm 42.

A Prayer Pair

Photocopy and cut apart these prayers.

Prayer 1
Religious Person

You're one of the most important people in your community, and everyone (including you) knows it. You have a reserved seat at church, and you're one of the largest contributors there. You know that God loves you—who wouldn't? You pray every now and then, and you're sure that God looks forward to each occasion just to hear the sound of your voice.

With this in mind, dramatize the prayer below. Feel free to "ham it up"!

"Dear God, I thank you I'm not like other people. I'm not like the drug dealers, the cheaters or even like that nerd over there. God, you know how much I do for you—all the contributions and all. I'm glad we're on the same team, God. Amen."

Prayer 2
Nerd

You're one of the least-popular people in town, and everyone (including you) knows it. You don't really pray much, mostly because you don't feel worthy to talk to God. You don't know what to think about yourself, but you know you need God a lot more than God needs you.

With this in mind, dramatize the prayer below.

"Oh God, please listen to me. I know I haven't done much to deserve your help lately, but I believe in your promise to love me. I'm sorry for the wrong I've done. Help me do better tomorrow. Amen."

Seven Tips for Prayer

There are about as many ways to pray as there are people. What works for me might not work for you or for cousin Fred. Here are some hints that may help you in your prayer life. But remember—the best way to be a better "pray-er" is to practice!

1 Make a habit of having a prayer time at the same time every day.

2 Speak in everyday language. God doesn't require "thees" and "thous" from us.

3 Pray whenever you need to talk to God. Silent words are just as effective as audible ones.

4 Pray about different things. Praise God for who he is; thank God for what he's done; tell God how you feel; ask God for what you need; confess what you've done wrong.

5 Be honest and sincere. Don't try to flatter God with your words. Just tell him exactly how you feel. Let him help you when you're hurting.

6 Keep a journal of things you want to pray about regularly, and use it when you pray. Write when you see prayers answered.

7 Find a prayer partner—someone you can trust who'll share your feelings, joys and concerns. Pray with that person regularly!

Telling the Jesus Story

D uring Jesus' life, he emphasized preaching about God's love and teaching others about him. Paul and the other apostles also affirmed the importance of telling others about Jesus as they began the church and invited people to believe. With the Holy Spirit's help and guidance, people continue to tell the story of Jesus' love.

People differ on exactly how the message of Jesus should be told, but all Christians agree it should be told in some way. Giving young people the chance to explore the important work of telling about their faith is vital to their growth toward maturity in Christ.

Use this meeting to help teenagers understand the importance of talking about their faith with others and discover effective ways to do it.

Objectives

In this meeting kids will:
- explore why it's sometimes hard to talk about their faith;
- understand the biblical command to share God's Word;
- see how God has been a part of their past and present; and
- identify simple ways of talking about their faith with others.

THE MEETING

1 Candy for All—(For each person, you'll need a candy bar.)

As kids arrive, give every other person a candy bar, but tell them not to eat their candy bars. When everyone has arrived, tell the kids with candy bars that you expect them each to give away their candy bar to someone else. See what happens.

Some kids will give their candy bars away. Others will refuse. Still others will trade candy bars with someone else who also has one. After the experience, ask:

● **How'd you feel when I told the candy-bar holders to give their treats away?** (Angry, because I felt like you were playing a joke on me; excited, because I thought someone might give me a candy bar.)

● **Why did some people not want to give their treat away?** (Because they were selfish; because I wanted the candy bar for myself.)

● **How is this experience like sharing your faith in Jesus with others?** (Some people keep their faith to themselves; some people only share their faith with others who also believe.)

Say: **Having faith in Jesus is like having a tasty candy bar we can share with others. But we sometimes hesitate to share because we're afraid we'll be rejected. God gives us the strength to overcome our fears and share him with others.**

Give candy bars to people who don't have one, and let them enjoy their treats as you move on to the next activity.

2 Laying a Foundation—(You'll need tape and three sheets of newsprint. You'll also need three balloons, each with one of these Bible references written on it: Matthew 28:19-20; Matthew 9:35-38; and Matthew 4:19. For each group of three, you'll need a Bible, a marker and a photocopy of the "Faith Foundations" handout on page 88.)

Form groups of three. Give each group a Bible, a marker and a "Faith Foundations" handout. Tape three sheets of newsprint to the wall. Above each sheet of newsprint, tape a balloon with a scripture reference on it—which you prepared beforehand.

Have groups work together to match the three statements on the handout with the three correlating Bible verses written on the balloons. As groups finish, have them each write each statement on the newsprint under the reference they think it matches. When the groups are finished, discuss any differences between the groups' answers. Then read the passages and give the correct answers. Here are the statements and corresponding Bible references:

● Telling others about Jesus is mandated by Christ (Matthew 28:19-20).

● Christ motivates us to tell others about him because of the love he's shown us (Matthew 9:35-38).

● Part of following Jesus means telling others about him (Matthew 4:19).

Faith Map—(For each person, you'll need a sheet of paper and several different-color markers.)

Say: **It's important to recognize that we all come to church because someone in our past told us about his or her faith. Let's think about the ways God has been a part of our lives in the past.**

Give kids each a sheet of paper and several different-color markers. Have kids each draw a faith map—a time line beginning with their birthdate and moving to the present. Be sure they include today's date on the right end of the time line. Have young people each "chart" their life of faith by indicating "highs," when they felt particularly close to God and "lows," when they felt alone in the world. Have them mark the highs and lows by indicating what was happening to them personally. Be sure they mark life-changing events that affected their faith. If you have kids who don't have a personal relationship with Jesus, have them each indicate other kinds of "highs" and "lows" on their timeline, such as special relationships or a year of good grades at school.

After kids have completed their maps, form groups of four. Have kids each explain their map to their group. Allow time for kids each to tell their story of how they came to the place they are today.

Retelling the Story—(No supplies needed.)

Once kids have told their stories, have them each draw conclusions about how they came to know God. Have kids each answer these questions in their groups:

● **How'd you come to know God? Was it quick and all-at-once or slow and time-consuming?**

● **Was the message of Jesus told by someone you knew or a total stranger?**

After kids answer the questions, call everyone together and say: **We effectively tell others about Jesus when we combine three important elements: Christ's story, our own story of life with Christ and the circumstances of the person we're talking to.**

Have kids get back into their groups of three, and ask groups each to quickly role-play one of the following situations. It's okay if more than one group has the same role play. In each role play, have one person act as the person in need and the other two help that person by telling their own stories of faith. Move the groups quickly so they don't make the skits too complicated.

Here are the situations:

Situation #1
Two Christian friends are talking to a non-Christian friend whose boyfriend just broke up with her.

Situation #2
Two Christian friends are talking to a non-Christian friend who's failing three classes in school.

Situation #3
Two Christian friends are talking to a non-Christian friend whose parents just kicked him out of the house.

When groups are ready, have them each present their skit to the whole group. After the skits, ask:

● **How'd it feel to tell your own faith story in your skit?** (I was nervous; it was exciting.)

● **How was it like telling someone "for real"?** (Everyone was watching, so I felt really exposed; these situations could actually happen.)

• **What makes telling your faith most effective?** (Being yourself; showing the other person you really care, instead of just "cramming" the Bible down his or her throat.)

5 Clothespin Medals—(For each person, you'll need five or six wooden clothespins and a pen.)

Say: **Today we've talked a great deal about ourselves and our faith stories. It's great to hear all the stories of how God has worked to bring each person into relationship with him. Let's take time now to recognize each person's uniqueness in God's family.**

Give each person five or six wooden clothespins and a pen. On each clothespin, have kids each write a quality of someone in the room that makes that person effective at telling others about Jesus. Then have kids each attach that clothespin to the appropriate person. Tell kids they can only clothespin someone once. Watch for kids who have few clothespins, and write additional affirmation clothespins for them.

6 Clothespin Closings—(You'll need a piece of string long enough to stretch across your meeting room. For each person, you'll need three wooden clothespins and a pen.)

When kids are finished, say: **Each of us is unique in God's eyes. Many people we know don't know God, yet they also hold a special place in God's heart. Let's close by praying for them specifically.**

Give kids each three wooden clothespins. Have them each write the names of three people they want to tell about Jesus. Have kids write each name on a separate clothespin.

Tie a string across the room so that it resembles a clothesline. Have kids each come up one at a time and clip one clothespin on the string, then say a one- or two-sentence prayer for God to help them share Jesus effectively tell that person about Jesus. Continue having kids pray until each person has prayed three times. Then close by thanking God for hearing kids' prayers.

by Scott C. Noon

Faith Foundations

Match these statements with the scriptures listed on the balloons.

Telling others about Jesus is mandated by Christ.

Christ motivates us to tell others about him because of the love he's shown us.

Part of following Jesus means telling others about him.

Faith in Action

The challenge to serve others resounds clearly throughout the Bible. Jesus gives countless examples of service and calls us to do likewise. The opportunity to put our Christian faith into action opens new doors of understanding and growth for adults and young people alike.

Kids who learn the value of serving discover new dimensions in their faith and often restructure their priorities to encompass a greater world view. They see there's more to life on Earth than just fulfilling their own needs and desires.

Use this meeting to help kids see how serving others imitates Christ and helps them feel good about themselves and God.

Objectives

In this meeting kids will:
- respond to how it feels to be served;
- evaluate how much time they spend serving others;
- identify people who need help;
- discuss why God calls us to serve; and
- commit to a service project.

THE MEETING

1 **Serving the Masses**—(You'll need soothing music and something to play it on. For each person, you'll need cookies and something to drink.)

As kids enter, have them get comfortable. Play soothing music in the background. Serve kids cookies and something to drink. Be kind and courteous, going out of your way to talk to everyone.

After you've talked to each person, turn off the music and ask:

● **How'd it feel to be served as you came in?** (Strange; warm.)

● **How would you rate my service—from 1 to 10, 10 being best?**

● **What made this service special or unusual?** (It was unexpected; it felt weird for you to serve me, since you're the leader.)

● **Within the last 24 hours and not counting my service to you right now, when is the last time others served one of your needs? What'd they do?**

2 **Scheduled to Serve**—(For each person, you'll need a photocopy of the "Time to Serve" handout on page 94 and a pencil.)

Give each person a "Time to Serve" handout and a pencil. Have kids each complete their handout by writing what their typical week's activities include. For example, in one week kids might spend:

● 35 hours in school;
● 5 hours doing homework;
● 1 hour in worship;
● 2 hours at a youth group meeting;
● 6 hours on the phone with friends;
● 10 hours eating;
● 42 hours watching television;
● 60 hours sleeping;
● 2 hours cruising;
● 4 hours with boyfriend or girlfriend; and
● 1 hour talking with parents.

Once everyone's list is complete, draw an imaginary line down the middle of the room. Explain that one end of the room represents zero hours and the other end of the room represents the entire week—168 hours. Have kids each total the hours they spent doing something for someone else in the last week (schoolwork doesn't count). Have them stand on the appropriate spot on the line that represents that amount of hours.

Ask for volunteers to share what they did to serve others. Affirm kids' actions.

Next, have kids each total the hours others spent serving them in the last week. Have kids each stand on the appropriate spot on the line that represents that amount of hours. Ask how others served them, and thank kids for their responses.

Say: **It's good for us to know how we spend our time. To-day we're going to explore the issue of serving and the role it should play in our daily lives as Christians.**

 Progressive Play—(You'll need a marker, newsprint and tape.)
Write these conditions on a sheet of newsprint, and tape it to the wall:

- hungry
- poor
- depressed
- helpless
- sick
- imprisoned
- lonely

Tell kids they're going to create a scene to act out all these conditions. Ask two volunteers to act out the scene kids create. Then have kids work together to decide each of these parameters:

- Location (must be outside);
- Time of year;
- Relationship between the two people (friends, brothers, husband and wife, or some other relationship); and
- Subject of conversation (you judge whether suggested subjects are appropriate).

Number the volunteers 1 and 2. Explain that they'll be doing an improvisational skit, with the rest of the group acting as directors. Tell the volunteers that every 30 seconds during their performance, you or another director will call out a volunteer's number and a new condition from the newsprint list, such as "#1—poor" or "#2—lonely." Then that volunteer must immediately assume that condition without stopping the skit. To begin, assign volunteer #1 as hungry and volunteer #2 as depressed.

Tell the volunteers to assume their characters and start talking. Every 30 seconds, have a different director change a volunteer's condition. Continue until each volunteer has changed conditions three or four times. Make sure all the conditions are covered in the skit.

After the skit, congratulate the volunteers and directors on their fun performance. Then say: **We laughed through this skit, but each of the conditions the volunteers portrayed are serious and sad. Let's think about how we can serve others who deal with one or more of these problems.**

Examine the Possibilities—(You'll need tape, newsprint, a marker and a Bible.)

Tape a sheet of newsprint to the wall. Have kids brainstorm ways they could serve people who have the different conditions covered in the skit. Write kids' responses on newsprint. Some examples might be: "I could talk to new people who come to my school and make them feel welcome"; "I could help out at a soup kitchen that feeds the hungry"; or "I could help tutor a failing student."

Make sure kids' answers are practical. Someone may suggest buying a poor person a home, but that probably isn't possible for most teenagers. Encourage kids to think of things they could actually do.

After kids share, say: **These service ideas would make people in need feel special and meet needs in their lives. But it'd also take up time we might want to spend doing other things.**

Ask:

● **Why should we consider doing these things for others?** (It makes people feel good; we need to help each other.)

Read aloud Matthew 25:31-46. Ask:

● **Why does God want us to serve others?** (When we serve others we serve God; God wants us to be like him.)

Media Service—(You'll need magazines.)

Distribute magazines to kids. Have kids sit in a circle, thumb through the magazines and read the ads. Go around the circle and let kids each tell about the services offered by one of the ads in their magazine. For example, a car ad may offer dependability, a smooth ride, comfortable seating or an affordable price.

After everyone has explained an ad, ask:

● **Would the services you listed from your ad convince you to buy the product? Why or why not?** (Yes, a dependable car would help me get around; no, comfortable seating isn't that important to me.)

● **How are the services offered in these ads the same as or different from the kinds of services we listed earlier?** (They're different because they have to be bought; they're alike because they each meet a need.)

Say: **TV and magazine ads would have you believe you can serve yourself and be happy and content for the rest of your life, but we know that isn't true. True service that really makes a difference in our lives goes much deeper.**

6 **I Choose to Serve**—(You'll need the service list from activity 4. For each person, you'll need a 3×5 card and a pencil.)

Give kids each a 3×5 card and a pencil. Have them each choose one service project to work on. It can be one from the list created in activity 4 or a new one they've just thought of.

Say: **On your card, write what you're going to do. Make it specific and include a completion date.**

7 **Service Sharing**—(You'll need a Bible, a sheet of paper and a pencil.)

Form a circle, and have kids each read their card aloud. Then read aloud James 2:14-18. Close by asking God to bless kids' acts of service.

Encourage kids each to keep their card as a reminder to serve. On a sheet of paper, write each person's name and deadline date. On each young person's deadline date, call to see whether the task is completed. Encourage kids to stick to their commitments.

by Karen Ceckowski

Time to serve

In the chart below, write all the things you do in a week and how much time you spend doing each one. Remember there are 168 hours in one week.

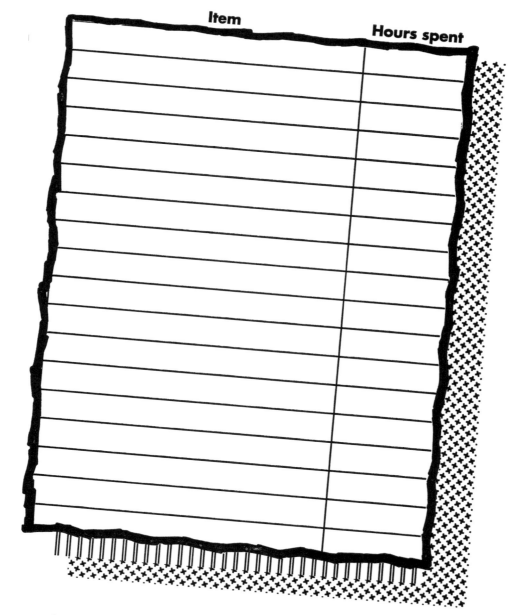

Item	Hours spent

Eternity With God

K ids are naturally curious about the future. They want to know what they'll do after high school and college, who they'll marry, what kind of job they'll have and how much money they'll make. They also want to know what will happen to them when they die, how the world will end and what heaven and hell are like.

But beyond simple curiosity, many kids are also afraid of what's ahead. Today's teenagers live with threats of nuclear war, AIDS, violence, world hunger, overpopulation, diminishing natural resources and—more immediately—failing grades in trigonometry.

Many don't realize God has already told us a lot about the future in his Word.

Use this meeting to help teenagers discover much of what God has told us about the future. The meeting will also encourage kids to respond to God's invitation to spend their future with him.

Objectives

In this meeting kids will

- illustrate people's preoccupation with the future;
- explain four aspects of the end times;
- discover what heaven and hell will be like; and
- respond to God's invitation to spend the future with him.

THE MEETING

1 **Newspaper Montage**—(You'll need newspapers. For each group of three or four, you'll need scissors, tape and a sheet of newsprint.)

As kids arrive, direct them each to make a newspaper montage. Form groups of three or four. Have kids each look through the newspapers and cut or tear out anything that deals with the future: articles, headlines, predictions, movie ads, ads for personal readings or horoscopes. Instruct the groups to tape these to a sheet of newsprint, making sure all the clippings are readable.

Give groups a three-minute warning to quit cutting, tape the clippings and choose a spokesperson to show their montage.

Have each spokesperson tape the group's montage to a wall and explain it. Ask:

● **Why is the future so interesting?** (Because it's so mysterious; because it's exciting.)

● **What excites you about the future?** (Thinking about what kind of job I'll have; wondering what my family will be like.)

● **What scares you about the future?** (Wondering what condition the environment will be in; wondering if I'll ever fight in a war.)

Say: **Everyone's interested in the future, but most people don't really know what'll happen. However, God's Word tells us some things we can know for sure. Today we're going to explore four specific future events.**

2 **Future Newscast**—(You'll need a photocopy of the "Future Features" handout on page 99, paper and pencils.)

Form four newscast teams. Give teams each a section of the "Future Features" handout, paper and pencils. Have teams each read their scripture and prepare a newscast segment on their subject. They may choose to do a news story reporting the facts, an opinion or editorial feature, an interview or any other kind of segment on a TV newscast. Encourage kids to be creative, but make sure they don't change the facts. The whole team must participate in the newscast. Kids can act as newscasters and field-reporters, and they can also be props such as a desk and chair, a map, a wall, a door or even a microphone.

When teams are ready, have them each present their newscast segment. Applaud each team's efforts, and take time for any questions kids have as a result of the presentations. Then ask:

● **How'd you feel as you listened to the newscasts?** (Worried; scared.)

● **Which newscast frightened you the most? Explain.** (The one about heaven and hell, because I wonder whether I'll make it to heaven; the one about the end of the world, because I'm scared of a nuclear war.)

● **What's something new you've learned about the future that you didn't know before this activity?**

● **How should this information affect the way we live?** (We should work at being like Jesus, because nobody knows when Christ will return; we should tell others about Jesus, so they won't have to go to hell.)

 Future Endings—(No supplies needed.)
Say: **God tells us that after we die, we'll spend eternity in one of two places: heaven or hell. We know heaven is a wonderful place—beyond comprehension! But what'll it be like for those who go to hell?**

Have kids form a circle. Walk around the circle and pull out every fourth person. Then have kids in the circle give each other back rubs while the other kids watch. If the other kids try to give each other back rubs, don't allow it and say: **You have to be in the circle to get a back rub. You can't have one.**

After about a minute, ask:

● **How'd you feel when I didn't let you get a back rub?** (Angry; rejected.)

● **How'd you feel as we received a back rub, and you were left out?** (Frustrated; like I didn't count.)

● **How are the people who didn't get back rubs like people in hell?** (They'll never experience the pleasure of "a back rub"—heaven; they look longingly at what might've been if they'd made the right choices.)

Have the rest of the kids give each other backrubs and say: **Being left out of this experience was bad, but it'd be far worse to be left out of heaven. You each still got a back rub. But once you die, there are no second chances.**

4 Invitation From God—(You'll need Bibles. For each person, you'll need a photocopy of the "God's Invitation" handout on page 100.)

Read aloud John 14:3. Say: **God wants us to spend eternity with him in heaven. He doesn't want us to go to hell.**

Give kids each a "God's Invitation" handout. Let kids read the front. Then explain Christ's gift of eternal life listed on the inside, explaining and expanding as necessary. Be sure to have volunteers read aloud the scripture.

5 RSVP—(For each person, you'll need a pencil and a photocopy of the "God's Invitation" handout on page 100.)

Give kids each a pencil. Have kids each read the "RSVP God" page from the "God's Invitation" handout and respond by checking the appropriate box. Have kids each write their name on their invitation. Collect the invitations once kids have responded so you can follow up with individual kids later. Invite kids who'd like to accept God's invitation now or would like more information to talk with you after the meeting.

6 Future Blessings—(No supplies needed.)

Have kids form a circle. Say: **Turn to the person on your right and say, "I want to spend the future with you because . . ." Complete the sentence with a positive remark, such as "because you're fun to be around" or "because you make me feel special."**

Have kids go around the circle and repeat the process until everyone has completed the sentence.

Close with prayer, thanking God for not leaving us guessing about the future and for wanting to spend eternity with us.

by Lin Johnson

FUTURE FEATURES

Photocopy and cut apart these sections.

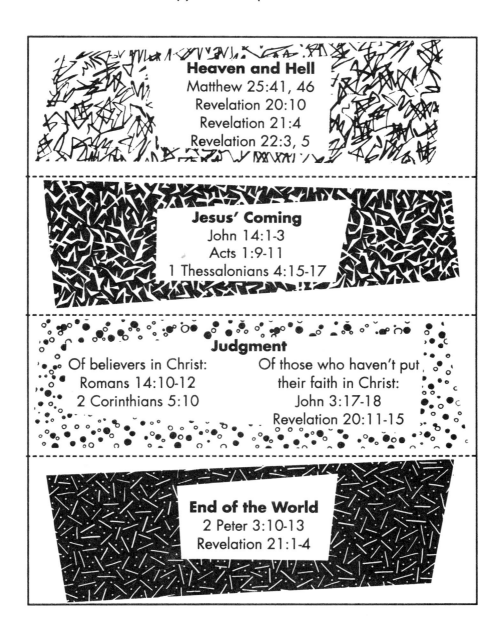

Heaven and Hell
Matthew 25:41, 46
Revelation 20:10
Revelation 21:4
Revelation 22:3, 5

Jesus' Coming
John 14:1-3
Acts 1:9-11
1 Thessalonians 4:15-17

Judgment

Of believers in Christ:
Romans 14:10-12
2 Corinthians 5:10

Of those who haven't put
their faith in Christ:
John 3:17-18
Revelation 20:11-15

End of the World
2 Peter 3:10-13
Revelation 21:1-4

God's Invitation

Photocopy, cut out and fold an invitation for each person.

God says . . .
- I love you and want you to have eternal life (John 3:16).
- However, you're a sinner and your sin has separated you from me. Death is the penalty for your sin (Romans 3:23; 6:23a).
- But my son Jesus paid the penalty for your sin (Romans 5:8).
- To have eternal life, you must put your faith in Jesus only (Ephesians 2:8-9).
- Once you do so, you can never lose your eternal life (1 John 5:13).

RSVP God
- ☐ I've already accepted God's invitation.
- ☐ Yes, I accept God's invitation now.
- ☐ I need more time to think about it.
- ☐ I'm undecided but would like to talk about it.

fold first ←

You're invited! Spend the future with me.

fold second ⬆